Boost Your Productivity and

Matt Avery

To Suze

Matt Avery is a former journalist, retail sales manager and marketing manager who runs two successful companies as well as writing and lecturing internationally on a number of topics. He also writes on work-related issues for several bestselling magazines. He has previously written a number of other business books including *Be Your Own Boss* (Hodder, 2010) and *Work for Yourself* (Hodder, 2011)

Boost Your Productivity and Achieve Your Goals

Matt Avery

Acknowledgements

My sincere thanks to everyone who contributed to this book with details of their experiences; and to those whose encouragement made it possible, especially my family, Victoria and Sam at Hodder Education, and Suze.

Contents

Introduction

Do you ever wish that you were more productive? Do you have a nagging feeling at the back of your mind that you could – and should – be achieving much more than you are? Do you ever feel overwhelmed with your workload and dissatisfied with your ability to manage it? If so, you're not alone – indeed research suggests that most people feel this way. With modern work practices people are increasingly feeling snowed under, caught in a downward spiral of having more and more things to do and less and less time in which to do them. As technology improves and more efficient methods of communication grow, it is unsurprising that we are never out of reach of work. And if we can't stem the tide of demands there is only one solution – we need to learn to become more productive.

For many people achieving their full productivity potential seems an elusive ideal – great in theory but difficult if not impossible to put into practice. They struggle with what seems like an enormous workload, continually firefighting tasks and only just keeping their heads above water. If this sounds familiar, then the good news is that it doesn't have to be this way, and boosting your productivity is easier than you think. It is perfectly possible to thrive with a massive workload and still remain calm, confident, relaxed and in control. If this sounds like a workplace Utopia, it's because it is – but it is a Utopia which is achievable. By implementing the tools and techniques in this book you can create a personalized productivity system designed to maximize your productivity in the workplace – and beyond it. By adopting these principles and undertaking the necessary changes in your day-to-day routines, your processes and your outlook, you can boost your productivity and keep it functioning at full power.

Imagine a world in which you can accomplish everything you need to, and with time to spare. Boosting your productivity allows you to do just that. To be more productive is to achieve more. And while you can't increase the number of hours in the day, if you can learn to become twice as productive then that's the equivalent of giving yourself twice as much time. You can even think of it as doubling your lifetime because you will be doubling what you can *achieve* in your lifetime. And it doesn't stop there. Maximizing your productivity is about reaching your full potential, which might mean you're increasing your productivity by three times, four times, or even more. Indeed, most people don't even know what their full potential is because they have never realized it.

So how can you boost your productivity so that you are able to manage all the demands put on you and remain on top of your work? Even enjoy it? The answer isn't to simply work longer and longer hours. In fact, this approach is completely counter-productive. Working longer hours often means that the quality of the output is impaired as you become tired, and because you are mentally and physically stretched it takes longer to accomplish each task – which serves only to tire you further. You will probably find that you do not have enough headspace to accommodate the things which really matter, and a lack of time and energy to do them justice when you do. And constantly living in this sort of pressure-cooker environment can ultimately be damaging to your health.

The answer to boosting your productivity so that you can accomplish everything with time and energy to spare lies in understanding what is impairing your productivity and understanding what changes you need to make. You will need to learn how to change your outlook, break any bad habits, plan and set about tasks, manage your time and resources... You will need to rethink everything you do from the perspective of maximizing your productivity and implementing a set of workplace disciplines that will allow you to retake control of your life. By managing every aspect of your life in the most efficient and effective way it is perfectly possible to deal with any number of tasks without becoming stressed or tired. Moreover, you will enjoy the very real benefits which come from being in control – of your workload, your time and energy, and – ultimately – your life. This book shows you how.

1

Barriers to Productivity – and How to Overcome Them

In this chapter you will:

▶ *Define the expectations others have of you in your work. Clarifying expectations will help you to boost your productivity by sharpening your focus*

▶ *Be clear about the finishing point – know when you have done enough*

▶ *Evaluate whether you are in the right job and able to reach your productivity potential*

▶ *Determine what needs to change in order to enable you to maximize your productivity, then do it*

▶ *Examine the options for changing jobs.*

How do you feel?

1 Do you know what exactly is expected of you in your job?

2 Is there an obvious and clearly defined finishing point to each project?

3 Can you fulfil your productivity potential in your current job?

4 Do you know what you need to change in order to boost your productivity?

5 Would you be more productive in a different job, or working for yourself?

The problem with poorly defined work

One of the principal barriers to achieving maximum productivity is disarmingly simple – a lack of understanding about what exactly our work entails. We can see the bigger picture and we understand what needs to get done and by when – a conference organized, a strategy defined, a project planned – but when it comes to buttoning down what *exactly* that entails the picture starts to become a little blurry. One of the problems is that what we have in mind may not be the same as other people in our organization. However, even that pales into insignificance compared to the reality that often we have no clear demarcation regarding what constitutes *completion* of the project. All too often we strive and strive to achieve perfection, often experiencing outside pressure to do so either from our bosses or from clients, when the truth is we may be breaking our backs to effect a minutely incremental improvement in the output. And putting in huge amounts of effort for a fractional gain is, clearly, an unproductive way to go about things. The trick is to know when to stop. Think about that for a moment – if it didn't happen, then nothing would ever be finished!

Let's take an example: car design and production. While it might seem a good idea, even the 'right' thing to do, for everyone involved in the process to strive for limitless perfection all the time, tweaking and re-tweaking endlessly in an attempt to continually refine and improve the output, the reality is that, if this were to happen without someone somewhere deciding when and where to draw the line, nothing would ever roll off the production line and the whole process would become academic. Cars wouldn't be manufactured because the designers could always find a way to marginally improve the car's aerodynamics or fuel consumption or reliability, or any one of a thousand other things, not least because, as the project went on and on, new materials and technologies would be discovered or become available. So the designs would never reach the manufacturing stage and car production would cease. Which would rather make the whole process obsolete. So we can see that it is vital to determine a cut-off point. However, such cut-off points are more often than not imposed on us. And that's where three significant problems surface:

1 If we have to complete a project in a **fixed, imposed timescale** but feel we must push ourselves continually to reach an undefined state of perfection in our work, we will simply be opening ourselves up to untold and limitless – and completely unnecessary and avoidable – pressure.

2 If we are unable to determine at the outset **the cut-off point** for our part of the project, then the woolly edges of our contribution will ensure that, because we do not know where to stop, we feel we never can.

3 By not knowing where we should stop – not understanding what constitutes **completion of our work** – we will never feel in control of the process or the output.

What we need to do therefore is to determine both the macro and the micro cut-off points:

▶ **Macro cut-off points** – these are the end of project sections, or the end of the project whole, which constitute the bigger picture and which are often imposed on us, such as the completion of a design or design stage so that the product can go into testing or manufacture.

▶ **Micro cut-off points** – these are the boundaries which determine a smaller piece of the puzzle, the piece with which we are directly involved, and are usually self-imposed. Indeed, they *should* be self-imposed so that we are in control of the output we will produce and the level of input required to produce it.

It is absolutely imperative that we determine *at the outset* what exactly the end result should look like so that:

▶ we have a clear picture of the **whole** of our work

▶ we know **precisely** what the work entails

▶ we know the **parameters** so we know with certainty when it is completed

▶ we know how much **time and effort** will be required and can plan accordingly

▶ we know when to **stop**.

Remember this: Know when to stop

This is not a way to give ourselves a ready-made excuse for being lazy nor a built-in reason why we can't achieve excellence in our work. It is simply a *vital requirement* in achieving *efficiency* in our work. If we are unable to decide a realistic limit to the amount of time and effort we should put in, then all our efforts beyond where the cut-off point should have been will be wasted.

Productivity in – and beyond – the workplace

Increasing your productivity does not need to be limited to work – indeed, the techniques described in this book can be applied just as effectively to your non-work life. Then again, define 'work'. For some people this means that nine-to-five routine; for others it is anything outside of their leisure time; and for some people it includes anything and everything which feels like a chore from their breadwinning occupation to doing the ironing, weeding the garden, or cleaning the car.

The truth is that no matter how you define work you can and should maximize your productivity across your entire spectrum. After all, what's the point of being wonderfully productive in one part of your life only for another to rob you of all the time and energy you've saved? Rather, the techniques and lifestyle changes which will enable you to exponentially increase your productivity should become a way of life. In this way, once you have got used to them, you will find that you hardly notice them, that they shape what you do and how you do it by running unnoticed in the background. All you will notice is that you are achieving much more than you used to, much more quickly, and much more efficiently.

Quick fix: Boost your productivity across the board

If you find that your productivity in increasing in your work but not in your home life, try adopting the same rules, techniques and principles there. It is perfectly possible to improve your productivity in all areas of your life simultaneously, and any gains in one area will naturally support the gains in the other.

Is your productivity diminished by your job?

One of the major barriers to productivity is a lack of enjoyment of, belief in, or motivation for the work you do. For many people their job and the day-to-day work it entails is a drag endured only because it pays the bills. Ask people whether they would continue in their job if it weren't for the money and many of them would answer with a resounding 'No!' Yet, if our work lives are unfulfilling, something is terribly amiss. After all, we spend a large portion of our adult lives working, so we need to ensure that we are doing something for which we feel valued and which in turn adds real value to our own lives – both in and outside of work.

If we do not, then there is a real danger that we will give up a sizeable portion of our lives to something which gives us very little benefit – or worse, something which takes more from us than it gives us in return. And if we are not excited by our work, then how can we realistically expect ourselves to be motivated by it? And if we lack motivation in our work, then it follows that we will almost certainly lack productivity – it is almost impossible to be truly productive unless we are enthusiastic, inspired and excited about our work and delivering to the best of our abilities. Far too many people suffer a shortfall in their productivity because they put up with a job which they perceive as one or more of the following:

- uninspiring
- unfulfilling
- undemanding
- unrewarding
- boring
- too hard

- pointless
- going nowhere
- not allowing them to fulfil their potential
- not what they want to be doing
- stuck in a rut.

The first thing to do is to examine your position and decide whether you are sufficiently motivated by your work and your work situation to be working as productively as possible. You will also need to factor in your life beyond your work – does your job hold you back from being as productive with your free time as you would like to be? Do you feel there is more you should be getting from your life but cannot due to the demands of your work? If this is the case, then you will need to re-evaluate your work life/home life balance, or change the demands of your work to allow you to fully realize the potential of your life outside of work.

Remember this: Get the right job for you

There has never before been a time when so many different jobs were available. The variety is staggering, with thousands upon thousands of career types, each offering something different and each with its own advantages and drawbacks. There really is something for everyone, so if you don't feel completely satisfied with your job then there is no reason – indeed, no excuse – not to explore other options.

If, having re-evaluated your work life/home life balance, you feel that your situation is holding you back in some way and preventing you from being as productive as possible, then you will need decide the best way forward for you. You can:

1 stay in your current job but **take steps to improve your situation** – and thus your productivity

2 **change jobs** to enable you to improve your productivity

3 **work for yourself** – where you will be solely responsible for your productivity.

We'll look at each of these in turn below.

Boosting your productivity in your current job

The first and usually simplest option is to remain with your current employer but take steps to improve your situation so that your job becomes something you really enjoy, something which fulfils your needs, and something at which you find being productive comes naturally. By just looking at the option of leaving your job, you have taken a significant step away from it and this distance affords you the benefit of gaining real perspective on your situation; so use this new-found insight to help you determine what it is you dislike about your current work life, what dissatisfies or disappoints you, what you feel is lacking, and what you feel you need to implement in order to achieve a more satisfying, rewarding and productive career.

Being productive at work is not just to the advantage of your employer (though this should not be overlooked) but something which will help you to enjoy your work more, to feel satisfied that you are achieving your potential. It will help both you and your employer by giving you the opportunity to get more out of your job and to give more in return. Having gained perspective and insight, you have a great opportunity to make any changes you feel are necessary, be they minor tweaks or major step-changes. Ask to have a meeting with your boss to discuss those elements of your work life which are preventing you from achieving your maximum productivity potential and need to change.

> 'My friend, saying that you don't have time to improve your thoughts and your life is like saying you don't have time to stop for gas because you are too busy driving. Eventually it will catch up with you.'
>
> Unknown

Use the following exercise to help you to determine what are the elements of your work life which are preventing you from achieving your maximum productivity potential and need to change. It will take some time to do this properly and will require some rigorous soul-searching to really understand what you want and need from your career for it to be really satisfying and meaningful – but it is time well spent.

Try it now: Improve your current job

First, draw up a list of all the things about your job which you dislike and which could reasonably be altered for the better. If you are a butcher, there is no point in saying that you do not like dealing with meat, but if it is one particular meat you find difficult or boring to work with, or if it is interfacing with the customers, dealing with the finances and so forth that is contributing to your lack of productivity, then perhaps there is a way to avoid, or at the very least to minimize, these in your day-to-day routine. Some of the most common negative aspects people quote in relation to their job are:

* feeling underpaid
* feeling undervalued
* being stressed
* operating in a poor working environment
* putting up with difficult working hours
* having a poor relationship with their boss or line manager
* having a poor relationship with their colleagues
* disliking the office politics
* finding the work unchallenging or boring
* feeling stuck in a rut
* not being able to see any future progression which inspires them
* feeling that they are not fulfilling their potential
* feeling that they are wasting their life away
* knowing that they do not want to be in the same position in ten years' time.

Of course, your list may be entirely different but it is likely that at least some of the above points will sound familiar – if not all of them! Once your list is complete divide it into three sections:

1 **'Crucial'** – those elements which simply have to change if your productivity is to improve and without which your work life situation will be untenable;

2 **'Secondary'** – the things you could live with or without if push came to shove but which would make a real difference if they could be addressed;

3 **'Would be nice...'** – all the other points, which are more niggles than real problems, but which would be so much for the better if fixed.

Next, draw up a second list, this time of all the things about your job in which you feel you are reaching you maximum productivity, or least have the opportunity to do so. Add to it those things which are not providing substantial barriers but which could be improved still further, and categorize them into three levels of importance just as you did with your first list.

Now draw up a third list – this is your wish list of all those things which, were they to be implemented (however unlikely), would allow you to reach your maximum productivity potential. Again, the goals need to be at least possible and if you have got an idea of timescale or ways in which your ideas could be incorporated then include these as well. Lastly, divide this list into three levels of importance just as you did with the other two.

By now you will have three lists, each divided into three levels of priority. The first thing to do is to put aside both the second list and those parts of the first and third lists which contain those elements which are of secondary and tertiary levels of importance to you. Do not throw them away because they will be useful to you at a later date, once you have sorted out those things which are your more immediate priorities. For now, though, you should concentrate your efforts solely on the primary sections of the first and third lists.

These detail all those aspects which are crucially important to you – those things which you absolutely must change in order for your productivity to improve significantly. They also detail those aspects which, if they can be implemented, will really boost your productivity so that your job becomes something you enjoy and not something you just tolerate – and you become better at it, achieve more and feel more worthwhile and valued in your work as a result.

By comparing the two primary sections of your first and third lists you can see at a glance the things which you feel really need to be improved and what the dream scenario for your job looks like. Next, you need to go through each of the points on these two sub-lists and try to determine how easy or difficult each is likely to be to implement and the timeframe over which any changes can be brought about.

Draw a simple two-axis graph on which to plot the points.

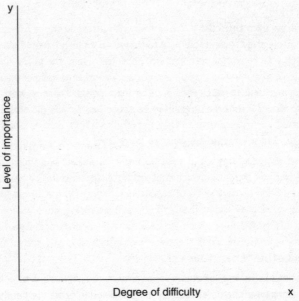

Figure 1.1

On the *x* axis chart the degree of difficulty (time and/or effort required) of achieving each of your aims and on the *y* axis rate the level of importance, so that something which you feel is crucial but difficult or slow to implement will be in the top right corner and something which is less important and easier/ quicker to implement will be in the lower left corner.

Now draw a line vertically down the middle of the chart and another horizontally across the middle, dividing the chart into four quarters. This determines your priorities and the order in which things need to be tackled:

- ► **The top left-hand corner:** This quadrant contains those elements which are most important to you and which are the easiest to tackle and quickest to implement. These should be your *first priority*.

- ► **The bottom left-hand corner:** This quadrant contains those elements which are quick and easy to implement but do not hold the same level of importance for you. However, bearing in mind that this chart only contains those elements which you rated 'Crucial', they still hold a high level of importance for you. These should be your *second priority*.

- ► **The top right-hand corner:** This quadrant contains those elements which will be difficult to achieve or will take a long time to implement but are nevertheless very important to you. These should be your *third priority*.

- ► **The bottom right-hand corner:** This quadrant contains those elements which are of a lesser importance to you and will take a long time to implement or be difficult to achieve. These should be your *fourth priority*.

Remember this: Keep reviewing your priority chart

This chart now contains all your requirements for boosting your productivity and the order in which they should be tackled but it should not be thought of as inflexible. Rather, it should be reviewed on a regular basis and added to or amended as necessary.

Now that you have clearly defined and prioritized all the changes you need to implement in your work life in order to allow yourself to maximize your productivity, you will need to ascertain the approximate lengths of time it will take to achieve each of them. This is important because it allows you to monitor the progress in your work life, thereby allowing you to see whether or not things really are improving in the way and at the speed you need them to. It is far too easy, having got this far, to feel that, by having identified all the changes that need to take place, you are halfway there to achieving them and that by starting the process of implementing the changes you will complete the picture.

Unfortunately, the reality is that each of your changes will almost certainly need to be carefully managed all the way through from implementation to completion, and identifying a timescale will ensure you can keep things on track. If, after a reasonable period of time, you look back at your list and realize that none of the changes have really taken place and that there is no good reason for this, then you will need to weigh up your options once more. If the barriers to your work life becoming as you need it to be are being created through foot-dragging by senior management, or, worse, by a concerted effort to deliberately introduce roadblocks which negatively impact your productivity, then you will need to consider the possibility that these changes will never take place and that perhaps leaving your job is the only way in which you will ever really gain genuine satisfaction from your career.

Change jobs to enable you to improve your productivity

If you have determined that remaining in your current situation is unlikely to allow you to implement the changes required to boost your productivity, you will need to determine whether it is likely, or even possible, that those elements of your work life which are a barrier to your productivity can be changed if you change jobs; and, if they can be, how long it will take to change them. Clearly, there is little point in simply switching employers if the productivity barriers are likely to be the same elsewhere. Equally, you need to decide whether or not those things which you would love to see in your work life are realistic and, if so, how long they would take to implement.

The following exercise will help you to draw a clear picture of your situation.

Try it now: Assess your current situation

First, make a list of the major barriers to productivity in your working life – those things you feel would need to be different in your next job in order for it to make the necessary difference. Try to limit your list to a maximum of about ten items.

Now draw a simple two-axis graph on which to plot the points you have identified. On the x axis chart the degree of difficulty (time and/or effort required) of achieving each of your aims and on the Y axis rate the level of importance, so that something which you feel is crucial but difficult or slow to implement will be in the top right corner and something which is less important and easier/quicker to implement will be in the lower left corner.

Next make a list of all those things which would be introduced into your work life, not in an ideal world, but in a better *yet still realistic* world, in order to boost your work life productivity. Again, try to limit your list to a maximum of about ten items. Draw another chart identical to the one you have just completed and plot the points accordingly.

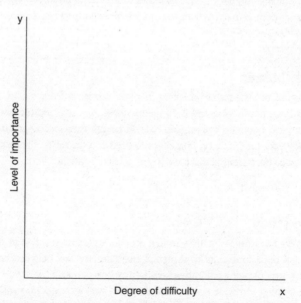

Now draw a horizontal line across both charts and ignore everything in the bottom half. If they are not sufficiently important to you to have made it into the top half, then they really should not influence your

'Should I stay or should I go?' decision. Of the remaining points on each chart, how many are on the left-hand side and how many on the right? What is the percentage difference between the two?

If the vast majority in the first chart are in the top right-hand corner, then most of the aspects which are really important to you and would need to be improved to make your current working life tenable are very unlikely to be achieved any time soon (if at all), and, even if they were, the process is likely to be drawn-out and painful. Likewise, if the majority in the second chart are in the top right-hand corner, then most of the new elements you would like to see introduced to give you the work life and productivity potential you desire are very unlikely to happen, at least any time soon. Thus, if the majority of the points you have identified as needing to change, improve or be introduced are in the top right portion of your charts, it may well be time to move on.

Now you are armed with the essential information regarding what it is that is holding you back from maximum productivity and the steps you will need to implement in your new job to make sure they are eradicated.

Myth-buster

Do not fall into the trap of thinking that you can reach your maximum productivity potential simply by implementing the tools and techniques in this book if you are in a job you hate. Although they will help you to improve your productivity, whatever the situation, you will only be able to reach your full potential if the work you do really satisfies you.

Case study

'You have two choices in life – to live your own life and reach your own potential or to contribute to someone else's dreams and help realize theirs. I am not being pejorative here – for some people a life's work is about helping someone else's cause that they feel a connection with. So be careful to make your choice – this is the easiest time in history that anyone has been able to express themselves and realize their own dreams – so make an informed choice.'

If you feel that moving on is the best option for you then the next decision is whether you opt to move to a similar company and work in a similar field or use this useful re-evaluation of your situation as the spur to move on to something completely new. This will depend largely on a great many factors which influence, directly or indirectly, your ability to reach your maximum productivity potential – this was, after all, the reason for your desire for change in the first place. Whatever you decide, you will be taking positive action to rectify a poor situation and that, surely, can only be a good thing. On the other hand, if most of the points are in the top left-hand corner, then the things which matter to you most are reasonably easy to alter, perhaps even speedily, and staying put but with a better working situation (thereby enabling you to reach your maximum productivity potential) might be your best option.

If this is the case, then you will want to gather the low-hanging fruit first, so start working your way through the list from the top left-hand corner (the most important and easiest to achieve) to the bottom right-hand corner (the least important and most difficult to achieve). This way you will begin to improve your situation to the maximum degree in the shortest possible time.

Work for yourself...

If neither of the first two options seem as though they will be able to allow you to create a situation in which you can maximize your productivity, then the best option may be to start out on your own. Prior to taking the leap to becoming self-employed, however, it is important to understand the pros and cons involved. These will, of course, vary from person to person since different aspects of quitting your job and becoming self-employed will assume varying degrees of importance to each individual. Indeed, some aspects which might be a positive productivity change for one person might well be a negative change for another person and vice versa, such as working alone all day.

Try it now: Evaluate the positives and negatives

A good way to understand the implications to you and your future business is to **compile two lists**, one documenting the ways in which quitting your job and becoming self-employed will boost your productivity and the other documenting the ways in which the change might be negative.

It is imperative that you compile your lists as accurately as possible charting those factors which you predict will have a major bearing on your productivity, so take your time to ensure your lists are as comprehensive as possible. You might like to use the following table as a starting point but they must not be considered exhaustive since such lists can never be all things to all people. Instead, use them as a starting point to give you some food for thought, adding anything which you feel is relevant and deleting any points which you feel do not relate to you. You might even wish to swap some of the remarks from one column to the other!

▶ **Ways in which becoming self-employed might boost your productivity:**

* Doing away with the **commute**
* Working to your **own timeframe**
* Working **when** and **where** best suits you
* No more worrying what **your boss** would think of *xyz*
* No more endless **calls on your time** to no value
* Being **tangibly rewarded** for hard work and success
* Increased **flexibility**
* Achieving a **better work/life balance**
* **Freedom**
* Being answerable and **accountable only to yourself**
* The feeling that **everything is possible** and that it is up to you
* The opportunity to pursue more **creative** and **imaginative** work interests
* The opportunity to work in a **broader field**
* New **challenges**
* Keeping all the **rewards** of your hard work
* An increase in **quality time** when and where it counts

▶ **Ways in which becoming self-employed might limit your productivity:**

✳ Need to **rely solely on yourself** – for everything in your work
✳ Lack of **defined** work structure
✳ No more **administrative support**
✳ Loss of a circle of **colleagues** who offer support
✳ Fear of the **unknown**
✳ Marching headlong **out of your comfort zone**
✳ Being faced with a **blank canvas** where is up to you (and destiny) to paint the picture – and your future
✳ **Isolation**
✳ **Loneliness**
✳ Loss of **IT** infrastructure/support
✳ **Financial** insecurity
✳ Loss of **external input/influence**
✳ **Risk**

Once you have completed your lists you will need to **assign a value** to each of your points, 10 meaning that it has or is likely to have a critical impact on your productivity and 1 meaning that it has or is likely to have little or no impact. Take your time over this because it is really important to determine exactly what is important to you in your working life in order to create an optimal environment for maximizing your productivity.

Then **reorder your lists** with the most important at the top and the least important at the bottom. Now get rid of everything with a value of 5 or less. What you are left with are those factors which have or are likely to have a critical impact on your productivity, the ones you should use in helping to determine whether or not taking the leap of faith to becoming self-employed is worth the risk and all the hard work it will entail. It will also give you a clearer idea of the framework you use to identify what it is about your work life which helps or hinders your productivity.

Quick fix: Tackle one problem at a time

If drawing up these lists and seeing everything you need or would like to change seems just too difficult, try breaking it down into smaller, more manageable chunks. Remember that you need only be tackling one problem at a time to be making progress.

Case study

'Originally, I wasn't thinking about going self-employed at all but after having job interview for a few companies nothing seemed right and a thorough analysis of the situation led me to conclude that working for a company where I wasn't in charge would always prevent me from achieving my full potential. The truth I realized was that I wasn't being 100-per-cent productive because I didn't care 100 per cent what happened – after all, I wouldn't get the rewards of my labours. That all changed as soon as I was working for myself and now my productivity is right up there.'

If your lists suggest that the downsides to going solo outweigh the upsides, then you will need to think long and hard about whether your expectations of becoming self-employed and the positive effect they will have on your ability to be more productive in your work are realistic. If you still think that they are, then revisit the lists to see which of these factors you would be willing and able to reprioritize.

Be careful to be completely honest with yourself here, though – it is far too easy to let a desire for a major shift in your work life in order to create that longed-for ability to reach your maximum productivity potential blinker you to the realities of becoming self-employed; ignoring the downsides now because you wish that they were not true or that they did not apply to you can prove to be a costly mistake.

However, if your lists suggest that the pros to becoming self-employed outweigh the cons for you, in all those areas where it matters most, then becoming self-employed might be exactly what you need in order to maximize your productivity.

Next step

Now that you have evaluated your current situation – and your priorities for making changes to it – let's now look at the main ways in which you can maximize your productivity ... and achieve that elusive work/life balance.

2

The Principles of Maximizing Your Productivity

In this chapter you will:

▶ *Develop the ability to focus on just one thing at a time*

▶ *Set limits to the amount of work you take on*

▶ *Create the optimum working environment*

▶ *Evaluate whether or not working from home is a practical option for you and how to use it to boost your productivity*

▶ *Maximize your efficiency.*

How do you feel?

1 Does your work life structure aid or hinder your ability to focus?

2 Are you taking on too much work to enable you to be truly productive?

3 Does your working environment inspire productivity?

4 Does working from home allow you to be more productive?

5 Is your work space set up to maximize your efficiency – and thus your productivity?

Learning to focus

A **positive mental attitude** is key to reaching your full productivity potential. After all, if you don't believe you can achieve what you want to, then there really is very little chance of making it happen. However, believing in your ability is, clearly, only part of the story. It is your ability to channel your thoughts to achieve a clarity of vision that will enable you to boost your productivity by allowing you to focus 100 per cent on the task ahead. If part of your brain is concerned with all the other tasks which need to be achieved, or with a nagging doubt that this isn't really what you ought to be doing, that there are more immediate tasks which need to be dealt with, then two things will almost certainly occur:

1 You will rush the task at hand;

2 Your ability to perform it will be impaired regardless of the time spent since your focus will be divided.

A by-product of this unfocused approach is that you'll be wasting an awful lot of energy:

▶ Thinking about the other tasks you need to complete takes energy;

▶ Trying to work out whether this is the task you should be focusing on at any given time takes energy; *and*

▶ Worrying about whether you're doing the right thing takes energy.

All of which means you are spending energy in a variety of ways which are not at all helpful, and all energy expended like this is energy which can't be directed to the task at hand. So being clear in your own mind that whatever it is you're tackling is exactly what you ought to be tackling is paramount to ensuring that you tackle it in the most efficient and effective manner possible.

Quick fix: Focus on the most important task

If you find it difficult to focus, or to know where your focus should be, try to determine what is your most important work, and then think about all the other things which might get in the way. Then picture a soundproofed glass case and very deliberately put all the possible distractions and calls on your time inside it and picture yourself firmly shutting it. All these other things you will have to deal with at some point will still be there when you need them, but for now you are free to concentrate only on your primary task.

Setting limits

Whatever your job and whatever your situation, it is of course true that you only have a certain amount of time and energy to give to your work each day. It is equally true for most of us that the demands placed on our time and energy outstrip our limited, and finite, resources. Every day we receive a torrent of emails, phone calls, letters, notes, instant messages, news, requests for information or assistance, etcetera, etcetera, and if we try to fulfil them all we will quickly sink under the volume of the work. In addition, our stress levels will soar and our enjoyment and satisfaction of our work will plummet.

How demoralizing it is, and yet how common, to end the day with an inbox just as full as it was when the day began; to realize with a sinking heart that the number of requests fulfilled is fewer than those demanded of us and that we will begin the next day with a fuller workload than we began this one. Clearly, this is unproductive and even dangerous, because living in this pressure cooker of stress and demands cannot help but take its toll on us over time. And the quality of our output will also be badly affected. It is therefore imperative that we learn to set limits:

- on the **amount** of work we take on

- on the **time** we devote to it

- on the level of **energy** we give to it

- on the **resources** we devote to it

- on the degree of **stress** we allow our work to put us under.

This will not only improve our work lives but also the quality of our work.

A good way to imagine it is as a goldfish bowl sitting underneath a dripping tap, with another tap at the bottom of the bowl to let out the water:

- The water dripping into the bowl represents the amount of work we are being asked to do;

- The tap releasing the water at the bottom of the bowl is the work we accomplish;

- The bowl itself is our capacity, in terms of both time and energy, to get our work done.

In an ideal world we would begin each day with the bowl empty, then, as the tap filling it dripped in our work, we would be able to open the outlet tap to the same degree. Our work would therefore never build up since we would be completing it at the same rate as it was arriving.

The situation all too often, however, is that the day begins with the bowl already half full (or more) and as soon as we arrive at our desk and switch on our computer we release an influx of work equivalent to turning the inlet tap fully on and immediately our bowl is full – or, worse still, overflowing. We are immediately thrust into panic mode, desperately trying to open the outlet tap sufficiently to deal with the influx. However, all too often it's impossible – we can only open our tap so far.

So how can we change the situation from one which is limiting our productivity by presenting us with a scenario in which we can't cope with the demands of our workload to one in which we are in control and able to deal with the work in a controlled and timely fashion without it getting on top of us? In other words, how can we use this model to help boost our productivity? First, let's look at the physics of this model to see what can and can't be changed:

Can't be changed

▶ The outlet tap can only be opened so far – there is only so much work we can get done, either directly or through delegation.

▶ The bowl has a finite capacity – there is only so much we can take on, only so much stress we can handle.

Can be changed

▶ The inlet tap can be regulated – the volume of work we allow into our lives, and the stress and pressure we accept being put under, can be changed.

Since the inlet tap is the only thing which can be altered, this is where we must focus our efforts. So how do we set about regulating the amount of work we take on?

Regulating the work influx

This is a **five-stage process** which should be used *regularly* – and not only when you feel you are beginning to drown in too much work. It is a good idea to use the following lists as a starting point and to add your own items as befits your personality and your situation.

FIRST STAGE

Identify the following:

▶ Where the work is coming from

▶ What of this work we must take on and what can be delegated or refused

- Your priorities
- Timescales for completion of the work
- How much time you have available.

SECOND STAGE

Understand why you take on too much work:

- Do you take on work simply because you are asked to, even if it might not be appropriate? Is this because:

  - you don't like letting people down?

  - you worry that it will look bad if you refuse?

  - you feel that you should be able to cope?

- Do you offer yourself for projects without really understanding the commitment?

- Do you find it difficult to resist getting involved with a piece of work which you think you will enjoy, even if you know you don't have enough time to do it?

- Do you say 'Yes' to every request for fear of missing out on a project which might prove lucrative, further your career, and so on?

THIRD STAGE

You need to understand why taking on too much work is detrimental to your productivity – and why limiting yourself to taking on the right amount is not laziness:

- Remember that taking on too much work:

  - splits your focus

  - costs you time

  - saps your energy

  - causes stress

  - is deeply unsatisfying

▷ prevents you from being able to complete the work to the highest standard

▷ is a guaranteed way to reduce your productivity.

▶ Remember that taking on the right amount of work:

▷ allows you to give the work your full concentration

▷ gives you sufficient time to complete the work properly

▷ energizes you

▷ ensures that you feel satisfied with a job well done

▷ prevents your work from becoming stressful

▷ allows you to complete the work to the highest standard

▷ is a guaranteed way to boost your productivity.

FOURTH STAGE

You need to decide which pieces of work you should accept and which you should refuse:

▶ What are your priorities?

▶ Are all the areas from which you are accepting work appropriate?

▷ Do you have to accept work from this source?

▷ Is there someone else better placed to deal with it?

▷ Is there someone else more appropriate to deal with it?

▷ Is the work beneficial to you and your career?

▷ Do you have the necessary time, energy and resources to take on the work?

▶ Will taking on the work prove detrimental:

▷ to your existing work?

▷ to your ability to take on other work?

▷ does the work have clear start and finish points?

FIFTH STAGE

Finally, you need to set, and action, limits to regulate the work influx:

▶ Ensure your line manager or work provider:

   ▷ knows your boundaries

   ▷ is aware of your other work commitments

   ▷ is clear about your career aspirations.

▶ Ensure that you know, at all times, how much work you are committed to doing and how much more you can take on. (This will help to make sure you do not take on more than you should, in a weak moment!).

▶ Know what resources you have at your disposal:

   ▷ time

   ▷ materials

   ▷ energy

   ▷ other people

▶ Be clear about the people to whom you can delegate:

   ▷ How much work can you give them?

   ▷ How often can you pass work on to them?

   ▷ What types of work can they do?

(N.B. Be careful you don't overload people through overenthusiastic delegation or *their* productivity will suffer.)

Once you have completed your lists you should have a clear understanding of:

▶ the work you currently take on

▶ the work you should/should not be taking on

▶ the reasons you take on too much work

▶ the type of work you can turn down or pass on

▶ how to go about it.

You should therefore be in a position to begin to action some of the steps you have identified as being important in order to regulate the workflow to ensure it is manageable, and the sooner this is done the better. Once the volume of work you are undertaking is appropriate, the quality of the output will soar as your productivity reaches new levels.

Remember this: Review your work influx

Your five-stage list should not be fixed. Instead, it should evolve organically over time, so be sure to always have it to hand and be prepared to update it as and when necessary. Try to get into the habit of reviewing it regularly and revising it as appropriate.

Creating the optimum environment

Crucial to maximizing your productivity is ensuring that you create for yourself the best possible working environment. This, of course, is a very personal choice and will vary from one individual to the next but can be broken down into three main groups:

1 WORK, WORK AND NOTHING BUT WORK

This is the focused, blinkered approach in which all non-work thoughts are dismissed, allowing you to concentrate solely on the task at hand. Some of the techniques employed by people who prefer this method include:

▶ surrounding yourself with workplace data

▶ equipping your desk/office with items associated only with your workplace

▶ having a calendar and schedule of your work prominently to hand

▶ purging your environment of anything not work-related.

2 THERE'S NO PLACE LIKE HOME

This is the approach taken by people who find that they work best when they feel least like they are at work. Some of the techniques employed by people who prefer this method include:

- surrounding yourself with photos of family and friends

- having mementos of family holidays, trips with friends, etc. prominently displayed

- employing a screensaver from your home life and a rolling photo frame of family, friends, pets, home, etc.

- keeping workplace data and communications to a minimum.

3 WHY AM I DOING THIS AGAIN?

This is the approach taken by people who find that they work best when they focus on the rewards that their work will bring them, the reason why they are putting in the long hours and covering the hard yards in the first place. Some of the techniques employed by people who prefer this method include:

- surrounding yourself with images of how you will spend the money your work is affording you

- having workplace deadlines prominently displayed together with a tangible reward you will give yourself once the piece of work is completed

- employing screensavers and desktop images of those things to which you most aspire and would buy if you had the money – e.g. expensive cars, luxury houses and dream holiday destinations

- keeping prominently displayed and thus front of mind those things which must be afforded and which your work will allow you to buy – e.g. kids' school fees, mortgage payments, credit cards and car loans.

For most people the ideal environment is a combination of approaches but one thing is for sure – finding and implementing the right one for you is key to maximizing your productivity. It has been said that you are a product of your environment –so take the necessary time to ensure that your environment is as good as it possibly could be for boosting your workplace productivity.

'You are a product of your environment. So choose the environment that will best develop you toward your objective. Analyse your life in terms of its environment. Are the things around you helping you toward success – or are they holding you back?'

W. Clement Stone

Effective home working

One additional and significant potential barrier to productivity which is becoming more and more commonplace is working from home. As more and more work is outsourced, communication technology improves, and commuting times and costs continue to increase, the number of people opting to work from home, whether or not they are self-employed, is steadily continuing to rise. This brings with it its own unique set of challenges in terms of creating and maintaining a workplace environment which will enable you to maximize your productivity. It stands to reason that, if working from home means you are subject to constant interruptions and your home life encroaches on your work life, then your workplace productivity will be impaired.

Remember this: Do a trial run

It may be possible to trial working from home to see whether or not it will work for you. This is a great way to dip a toe in the water and get a feel for it without fully committing yourself, but remember that to really see how well it would work you will need to create your environment with the same care as if you were fully taking the plunge.

It is also a common pitfall for those who choose to work from home that their working environment never truly feels like a work space, and as such making the transition from home life to work life can be extremely difficult. On the other hand, depending on your personality and your setup, working from home might allow you the freedom to create exactly the right working environment for you, aiding your productivity in a way which would never have been possible in a shared office. However, wherever you choose to work, creating the right environment will help to put you in the right frame of mind to tackle your work and is crucial in the quest to maximize your productivity. It is therefore important that your office should look and feel like a workspace – even if you choose to then decorate it in the "There's No Place Like Home" style.

Case study

'I have turned the spare room into an office. After the first year of being literally in the spare room, perched on the bed and using a dressing table as my desk, I decided to create a real office. It works very well. I have a glass door, nice chairs and a huge desk. It looks and feels like my very own office. Neither the product of some cost-conscious corporate "furnisher" nor a ludicrous glass-and-metal "designer" office that looks like a set from some tacky soap opera. It's mine and I feel very comfortable in it.'

How exactly you achieve this will depend upon a number of factors such as budget and time constraints but the following may provide a few useful pointers in ways to maximize the productivity with which your physical space can empower you:

▶ Turn any **permanent fixtures into practical office furniture** (e.g. fixed wardrobes into store cupboards).

▶ Decorate your office in **neutral tones** – just take your cue from any large multinational.

▶ Choose a room with a **plain outlook** (e.g. not onto the back garden where your kids will be playing much of the time).

▶ **Avoid furniture which doubles for domestic duties** (e.g. a sofa for those creative thinking moments which converts neatly into a bed for guests, thereby converting your office into the spare bedroom and denying you any bona fide workspace every time you have visitors).

▶ Go mad on **shelving** – nothing makes you feel like you have arrived at work like the sight of business books and box files.

- Invest in **filing cabinets** – this will help to keep your desk uncluttered as well as ensuring all your vital documents are always readily to hand.

- Install **lots of lights** (a well-lit office makes it easier and less tiring to concentrate for long periods (you never saw a dim office in a multinational).

- Fix **blinds** instead of curtains.

- **Keep artwork, ornaments and knick-knacks to a minimum** – and if they would look out of place in the office of a standard large corporate, then get them out of yours.

Remember this: Create an optimal working environment

Creating an optimal working environment is one of the most important things you can do to boost your productivity, but strangely it is one of the aspects of working from home which is often overlooked. Do not underestimate the importance of creating a working environment which puts you in the right frame of mind from day one, firmly putting you into work mode every time you arrive at your workspace.

So is working from home right for you? It largely comes down to a matter of whether you can effectively separate your work life from your home life and avoid the myriad additional distractions, which will be ever present, while maximizing the opportunities home-based working affords:

Barriers:

- the need to create your own day-to-day routine
- lack of defined work life structure
- lack of external stimulus
- a greater need for self-motivation
- a greater need for self-discipline
- ever-present distractions
- greater likelihood of interruptions emanating from your personal life

Advantages:

- ▶ the opportunity to create your ideal working environment

- ▶ work the hours and days which best suit you

- ▶ employ the best equipment and IT infrastructure for your situation

- ▶ easier to isolate yourself from constant workplace communications and interruptions

- ▶ the opportunity to employ your preferred working methods

- ▶ no one looking over your shoulder

- ▶ work where you want, when you want

With any luck you should be able to create your ideal working environment, and provided you are conscious of the many potential productivity pitfalls of working from home, you should be able to successfully navigate around them.

Case study

'When I had the opportunity to work three days a week from home in my current job I jumped at the chance. The thought of only having to suffer the commute two days a week instead of five was extremely tempting. In addition, I was convinced that working from home would work for me since I have never found self-discipline to be a problem. As soon as I started, though, I realized that I simply wasn't getting as much done working from home as I would have done had I been in the office. After much soul-searching, I realized the problem was not my inability to work from home per se but rather that I didn't have a suitable working environment at home. I immediately set about rectifying the situation and once I had an office which made me feel like I was at work the moment I stepped through the door my productivity went straight back to 100 per cent.'

Perhaps the single biggest challenge to their productivity any home-alone worker faces is the juggling of home life and work life, given that, by definition, these occupy the same space. It is therefore vitally important that you develop strategies to separate them – both for you and for anyone who lives with you.

Working at home can certainly take some getting used to and it is all too easy to underestimate the skills and determination required. The constant temptation to become sidetracked by home life coupled with the capacity for never-ending interruptions from family who think that because you are at home you are not working can have a serious negative impact on your productivity unless it is carefully managed – e.g. denying your family access to your office, and to you, while you are 'at work'.

Achieving the most productive work/life balance

The crucial task facing everyone who works from home and who can work their own hours in any configuration that pleases them is to work out a pattern which enables you to balance your work life with your non-work life to the best effect, not only for you, but for your business and your family, too. You will enjoy a great degree of flexibility in your work life, and this should also be carried over into your home life in order to boost your productivity to the maximum degree.

There are so many ways in which you could try to find the perfect balance but for most people it is a case of trial and error until they get it right. Remember to review the situation frequently and to discuss it with any relevant parties to make sure that it is working to the benefit of everyone involved. Just keep in mind that an imperfect work/life balance can be hugely detrimental to your productivity – but that getting the balance right can boost your productivity exponentially.

If you find that for some reason or another you are not getting the balance right and that your home life or your work life is suffering as a result, then you will need to re-examine the structure you have defined and try to pinpoint how and where it is not working. It should be relatively straightforward to determine which element of your life is too dominant and which is suffering, but creating harmony in the yin and yang of your work life/home life balance can be very challenging. However, it is achievable and will ultimately result in the potential to maximize your productivity. It can be difficult, though, especially at first, and if you are struggling then rest assured that you are not alone – a great many soloists find that this is one area which seems to be particularly problematic.

One of the reasons for this is that, if you don't have the framework of a paid job where the workday and workplace structure is immovable, then you need to set your own boundaries, boundaries which need to be negotiated with other members of your household whose priorities may well differ from yours! However, if your productivity isn't to suffer, then it's something which will need to be addressed, and if you approach the challenge in a methodical manner you should find that you can make it work to the benefit of all concerned:

1 Ascertain the optimum work/life balance for you, your family, and your work needs.

2 Determine which area is taking too much of the share, and to what degree.

3 Try to identify any patterns which are causing problems in creating the desired work/life balance and establish the reasons for this.

4 Identify the ways in which this imbalance is hindering your productivity.

5 With all appropriate parties, create an action plan to remedy the imbalance.

6 Put the plan into action and monitor the situation carefully. Be prepared to adjust as necessary.

One word of caution – it is very easy to allow your work to take too much precedence in your life even if it is only allocated an appropriate share of your time. This is because your work can unbalance your home life in a different way – mentally – by you never switching off, and this is a sure-fire way to impair your productivity. So it is very important to ensure that when you are working you focus on your work, and when you are not working you focus on letting go.

Home life versus work life – separation and synergy

You may well find that a significant portion of your time will be eroded by well-meaning visitors and this can pose a very real threat to your productivity; partners offering a cup of coffee which segues neatly into a 20-minute discussion about domestic affairs, or the children who descend on you and talk you into leaving your work to play with them, or the family dog who needs a walk, etc. And it's a real concern for every home-alone worker when they are not home alone because every valuable minute taken up with domestic issues is time stolen from the paid work you should be getting on with. In other words every minute stolen is a minute of potential productivity wasted.

To put this into perspective, try to imagine working for a large multinational and having your partner arriving at your desk to discuss domestic issues several times each day, then throw into the mix your children, friends, dog, etc. invading your office and demanding your attention. Putting yourself mentally back into the fixed workplace harness is a good way of seeing whether or not what is going on in your workspace is aiding or hindering your productivity. Large multinationals have over the years refined methods for increasing the productivity of their workforce. If you decide to work from home, you will need to do the same.

Case study

'My at-home office is the spare bedroom but when my partner and I agreed that I would be using this space we also agreed that I would be taking it over permanently. This is crucial to safeguarding my productivity since it means that I can have it decorated and furnished the way that best suits me to enable me to get the most from my work, and also because it means that I have a room in the house where I can go to be completely alone and focus 100 per cent on my work.'

Of course, allowing, and even creating, flexibility in your work/life balance is one of the bonuses of working from home and managed correctly it can indeed boost your productivity. But how do you go about achieving the optimum balance?

Time and space

TIME

There is really only one tried-and-tested solution to ensuring that your time is not eroded – you need to ring-fence it. People have of course tried all sorts of methods over the years but very few people can honestly say that they can maintain 100-per-cent productivity in their work lives without strictly safeguarding their time. So, agree simple rules with family members about when it is OK to disturb you and when it is not – and decide upon some firm boundaries for yourself. You might, for instance, ensure you always take a break for half an hour when the kids get home from school and build this into your work schedule – after all, regular breaks are necessary in order to maintain your productivity levels. But make sure it is understood by one and all that after your break you will not reappear until dinner time. This gives everyone access to you (and you to them) without any encroachment on your work time and without unnecessarily damaging your productivity.

Taking breaks when other people are around can in itself be a boost to your productivity since it can help to stimulate and energize you. Just how rigid you make the times of your breaks and how keenly you enforce the rule that you are not to be disturbed depends largely on your ability to manage the situation without compromising the needs of your productivity, but most home-alone workers find that clear boundaries not only make it easier for them to achieve the desired amount of daily work time, but easier too on the other members of the household since everyone knows exactly where they stand.

The other advantage is that just as this strategy prevents other people from diminishing your productivity by encroaching on your work time, so equally it shields you from doing the same thing by removing the temptation to spend more time with them than you should and to take more and more frequent, and longer and longer breaks. Overtly ring-fencing your time really is to the benefit of everyone.

SPACE

Since by definition every home-alone worker works from home, it is vitally important to establish a clear demarcation between your work space and your home space. Creating a clear and unambiguous physical definition of your workspace is crucial to putting yourself in the right frame of mind – entering your workspace should automatically put you mentally into 'work mode', crucial for maximizing your productivity.

If you are fortunate enough to have one room in your house which you can convert into an office, then it should be relatively simple; if your workspace needs to double as part of your life space, it can be a lot trickier. However, creating boundaries is key to safeguarding your productivity. Designating your office as off-limits whenever the door is shut is a great way to achieve this, and it is important to safeguard your productivity by having a sanctuary in which you can focus 100 per cent on your work.

Quick fix: A 'closed door' policy

To ring-fence your time, try adopting a 'closed office door' policy. Ensuring that you are not disturbed means ensuring that your productivity will not be diminished.

If your workspace is allowed to blend with your living space and your home becomes your office, then your all-important means of feeling like you have left home and arrived at work each day will quickly evaporate – and with it your productivity.

Remember this

If you do not take great pains to keep your home space and workspace separate, then one will simply disappear, and it will almost always be the workspace. Do not be fooled into thinking that it will blend seamlessly into a realm which is both delightfully tranquil and at the same time a hive of industry, where great work is achieved alongside great living. That is a Utopian dream of home working that is, unfortunately, rarely the reality – and if you don't successfully separate your home life from your work life, the biggest loser will very likely be your productivity.

Case study

'When I started working from home I decided to enjoy my new freedom to the full and stacked all my work on a small table next to my favourite armchair. Why work sitting at a desk when you can be more comfortable? Then I started watching television while I worked. It was great – until I realized that my productivity had halved (or worse) compared to working in an office. Now I sit at my desk to work every day and my productivity is back up to 100 per cent.'

Maximizing efficiency in your workspace

In order to ensure your work space doesn't get in the way of your productivity, it is important to create an environment which suits and reflects your taste and working style, whatever these might be. If you work most effectively in a clean and tidy workspace, uncluttered and functional, then that is how your office should be. If, however, you genuinely find you are more productive in a messy environment, things flung to the four corners of the room, then that is what you should create; but be honest with yourself – do not fall into the trap of convincing yourself that you work best in a state of perpetual organized chaos just so you have an excuse to never tidy! How many times have you heard people say things like 'It may look untidy to everyone else but I know exactly where everything is,' or 'I know it's a bit of a mess but that's how I work best'? And how many times has that person been you?!

The fact is that, while most of us do not keep our workspace as tidy as we should, we always feel a sense of relief, of renaissance even, each time we do get around to the big tidy – getting up to date with the filing, with the company accounts, cleaning and tidying the office, sorting our desktops (real and virtual) and so on. And every time we think the same thought: 'That's better! Right, I definitely won't leave it so long next time...'

Because the truth is that for 99 per cent of us a tidy and well-organized workspace will increase our productivity, allowing us to concentrate better and to more accurately focus our energies. So when creating and maintaining your working environment, be honest about your needs.

Next step
So now that you have learned a few basic principles that will help you to boost your productivity – managing your workload and creating an optimal working environment among them – we can now move on to looking at the way you actually work and approach tasks.

3

Simplification

In this chapter you will learn how to:

▶ *Multitask for maximum productivity and learn to keep track of all your commitments while focusing only on one*

▶ *Organize and prioritize your tasks*

▶ *Add flexibility to your work routines and capitalize on the freedom modern IT systems can provide*

▶ *Cut out the dead time and boost productivity through efficient working practices that utilize every spare moment*

▶ *Streamline your working practices and organize work efficiently to minimize the transition time between tasks.*

How do you feel?

1 Are you able to multitask effectively and productively?

2 Do you organize and prioritize tasks in the most productive way?

3 Could you utilize the capacity for flexibility in your work routines to boost your productivity?

4 Do you waste valuable time which could be used productively?

5 Are your work practices streamlined for maximum productivity? Why, exactly, do you want to be more productive?

An executive at a large multinational once told me that, despite making a number of changes to his work life and day-to-day routines in order to increase his productivity, he didn't seem to have any more time or energy as a result. Upon investigation it transpired that the reason was simple – as he had streamlined his working practices and increased his efficiency, so he had more spare time in his day-to-day working life, which he understandably felt he ought to put to good use. He therefore took on more and more projects and with them more and more work! So the fact was that he had increased his productivity and had generated for himself more time, but it was his inability to ring-fence and safeguard this new-found time which was causing him problems. He had indeed increased his productivity but as fast as he was digging a hole he was finding something with which to fill it.

Quick fix: Pinpoint your motivation

It's important to understand *why* you want to be more productive. Once you have a very clear understanding of your reasons you can use these as powerful motivation to help you to achieve them. What will you do with the extra time and energy your increased productivity gives you?

So it wasn't his lack of productivity which was holding him back but rather the way in which he dealt with his increased productivity. It is therefore vitally important that you are very clear about what it is you are hoping an increase in your productivity will achieve: Do you want to have more time and more energy for non-work pursuits, or do you want to be able to take on more work and get it done without adding to the amount of time you spend doing it?

Doing one thing at a time

How many of us can honestly say that our work entails doing just one thing at a time? Indeed, how many of us only need to do half a dozen things at a time? The truth is that increasingly people are being expected to juggle an enormous number of tasks, projects, work streams and communications of various kinds. For most people it is a depressingly familiar scenario to find that in the middle of trying to accomplish one task they are being expected to begin planning for a future task, update colleagues on other ongoing tasks, offer opinions on additional projects, and participate in a seemingly endless stream of round-robin email discussions.

Quite simply, this method of working, which is so common in today's workplaces, is a recipe for disaster. Every time you need to shift your focus from one task to another, however briefly, you are inadvertently doing two things:

1 **wasting time** as you mentally drop the first task and get your head round the second

2 **wasting energy** as each new task requires a fresh input of energy.

A good way of visualizing the wasted time and energy these interruptions cause is to imagine that you need to complete a car journey of let's say 10 kilometres. If you follow the principle of doing one thing at a time and not allowing yourself to become distracted, then you will simply get into your car, start the engine and drive the 10 kilometres. You'll arrive in good time, calm and unruffled, and with sufficient energy to tackle a new task – and you will have got your car from A to B as quickly as possible.

Not following this principle is akin to getting into your car, starting the engine and driving a few hundred metres before stopping the car, switching off the engine, getting out and getting into a different car. Then starting the engine and driving another few hundred metres before pulling over, switching off the engine and transferring to another car, and so on and so on. In order to complete your journey you might have to make 50 or more micro journeys, using 50 or more different cars and wasting huge amounts of fuel (energy) and time since you will have to fire up the engine afresh each time and then accelerate hard to get up to speed. You will also be wasting additional time and energy switching between cars. And by the time your journey is completed you will be exhausted – and late. Moreover, although you will have reached your original target destination, you can look back to see all the other cars you've used just fractions further on from where they were. So it is with your work.

Focusing on one thing at a time allows you to achieve it with the minimum of wasted time and energy and to take it right through to completion, ready to tackle another task. Flitting between tasks, however, slows you down, saps your energy, causes untold amounts of stress, and when you look back at what you have achieved you will see that it is very little – that each of the pieces of work you were distracted by have moved on hardly at all.

Remember this: Do the maths

By concentrating on just one thing at a time and devoting all your resources to that, you will achieve it in the most efficient manner possible, ready to move on to a new task. Think of it as completing ten tasks consecutively, each one taking 10 minutes – after 100 minutes you will have completed all the tasks. If you were to spend 5 minutes on one, then 5 minutes on the next and so on you might need to revisit each of them four or five times – taking a total of 200–250 minutes.

In my work life I am constantly engaged in a balancing act as I need to find the time to devote to a number of tasks. Typically, at any one time I might find myself writing a book, producing a show, and running my three companies. If I didn't set myself strict rules governing how I manage my resources, particularly my time and my energy, this would prove impossible. As it is, I can only devote, on average, one day per week to each of my enterprises. That day must therefore be made to work as hard for me as possible. As you can imagine, I would get nowhere fast if I tried to work on all five projects simultaneously and my productivity would reach an all-time low if I allowed any of the projects other than the one on which I am working on any particular day to encroach on my time.

I therefore begin each day knowing which of the five projects I will be working on and I limit myself to that project alone. As emails relating to any one of my other projects bombard me throughout the day I need to be disciplined to ignore them. Many people find this concept one of the most difficult to implement since it seems at first as though you are simply hiding from work and not being productive at all. The truth is, however, that those emails will still be in your inbox at the end of the day, and if anything is so urgent that it simply cannot wait, then you can be sure that whoever it is who is trying to get your attention will contact you in another way. Because of this I limit the number of people who have access to my work phone number and ensure that those who do understand that it is only to be used before 5 p.m. if there is a real emergency. Between 5 p.m. and 6.30 p.m. I take and make calls and answer my emails.

Even then, to ensure maximum productivity, I only answer the emails relating to whichever task I have been working on that day. To this end I find it best to have five different email addresses, and by only checking the relevant one each day I am not distracted and my focus is not split nor my concentration pulled in a number of different directions.

While your work situation will have a different and unique set of demands and challenges, the universal truth is that for 99 per cent of people there are a number of different elements competing for your time and energy every day. While your coping mechanism may therefore be different to mine, the principle is exactly the same – ring-fence your time and energy and cut out all distractions and interruptions which threaten to disrupt your focus. Concentrate on one thing at a time, and one thing alone, and work only on that to maximize your productivity.

Download – organize – action

In order to maximize your productivity you need to determine what you need to achieve, by when it needs to be done, the sequence in which tasks should be tackled, and to implement a system for doing it. This can be broken down into three sections – 'Download', 'Organize' and 'Action'.

1 DOWNLOAD

The first thing you will need to do is to compile a comprehensive list of all the things you need to achieve, and a realistic timescale of when they should be completed. Not only will this allow you to get them out of your head and onto paper – thereby freeing your brain up for more important tasks such as actually getting things done – it will also create a constant reminder of the tasks you face and ensure that nothing is forgotten or left out. This list should be *continually* updated, not once a week or even once a day but constantly, every time a new task is created or an existing one completed. Your list should always be an up-to-the-minute reflection of the needs and challenges you are facing in your work life, logically laid out and clearly presented, allowing you to see at a glance where you are, where you need to be, and by when.

2 ORGANIZE

The next thing you will need to do is to organize your list. Depending on the length and complexity of your list, this can take quite some time to accomplish but it really is worth putting in the effort to get it right at this stage since it will save you an awful lot of time, aggravation and wasted energy in the future.

Remember also that it will only be a protracted process the first time you do it. After that it will become organic, happening automatically as a result of the process of effective download since each new item added to the list should be inserted in the correct place straightaway. Remember that what you are doing is 'downloading' not 'dumping' – simply adding to your list in a random manner or adding to the top of your list with the intention of organizing it at a later date is a recipe for disaster.

3 ACTION

The final, but by far the most important, element is to action the tasks you have listed. Remember that creating lists can be a double-edged sword as it is all too easy to fall into the trap of thinking that just because the tasks are out of your head and on the list they have been taken care of. The reality of course is very different. Until the items have been actioned you haven't actually achieved anything – the 'download' and 'organize' elements of the process are merely tools (albeit very necessary ones) to enable you to action the tasks in the most streamlined and efficient manner possible. Therefore actioning the tasks is what it is really all about and, while this can be the most challenging part of the process, it can also be the most rewarding.

How to action your tasks effectively

There are, in fact, only **three ways** in which any and all tasks can be actioned. These are:

1 delete

2 do

3 delay.

These are in stark contrast to the myriad ways in which we can seek to avoid actually actioning tasks. These include:

- dithering
- dallying
- dawdling
- doubting
- dreaming
- drifting.

The trick is to make decisions as quickly as possible and then straightaway action them in one of the three viable ways. Remember that in this context "Delay" means delaying doing the task, not delaying making a decision about it. Deciding that you can't make a decision yet is often a safety behaviour used when we're anxious about making a mistake. It's completely understandable but facing this fear and pushing through it is vital if you are to really improve your productivity – it actually very seldom occurs that we really *can't* make the decision; it's rather that we don't *want* to. Of course, there are exceptions to the rule such as because you don't have all the information required to make an informed decision, or there are other people who will need to be consulted first, and in these cases you will need to be on your mettle to be extra vigilant that you don't allow your productivity to dwindle because you lack the necessary motivation.

Remember this: Be vigilant!

Beware falling into the trap of prevaricating by actioning the majority of the tasks you need to accomplish by putting them into the 'Delay' box. In fact this category should comprise by far the smallest portion of all the task actions – typically no more than 10 per cent. If you find that you are putting more than 10 per cent of your to-do list into the 'Delay' category, then you will need to revisit your organization and prioritization strategy and, crucially, you will need to go through all these tasks again to ruthlessly determine if they do in fact belong in either the 'Do' or 'Delete' categories.

Let's look at each of the action categories each in turn.

1 DELETE

The truth is that a great many of the tasks we have scheduled, or simply have at some point added to our inbox, should not be there. There are several reasons for this:

- ▶ They should never have been put there in the first place.

- ▶ They are tasks which in an ideal world would be great to action but which are not a priority and are unlikely to become so – and thus realistically they are unlikely ever to get done.

- They have been there in the 'Delay' category for weeks or possibly months and upon each revision of the list that is where they end up staying.

- Outside factors have changed since the task was added to the list and so it no longer needs doing.

- It can be delegated and so in effect will be joining someone else's list and can be deleted from ours.

It is crucial that you are **realistic** and **ruthless** every time you review the list. It is pointless leaving a task in the 'Delay' category (or even the 'Do' category) if deep down you know that for whatever reason it is something which is unlikely to ever be done.

Quick fix: Weed out unnecessary and unimportant tasks

If an item has been on your list for a long time without being either completed or deleted, then it is something which is unlikely to ever be done. And if it hasn't been missed in that time, then it is unlikely to be important anyway.

In the same way, if it is something which can be delegated, then it should be, and deleted from the list; and if it should never have been put there in the first place, then it is a clear indication that you need to become more rigorous with your evaluation of tasks. If they fall into the 'would be great but realistically I know it's never going to happen' category, then delete them. And because outside factors do change so will your list, so get into the habit of reviewing it often.

Quick fix: Short, relevant, realistic

Having an extensive list of things which need to be completed can be soul-destroying. The fewer the items on the list the more likely they are to be done. Remember that tasks which remain on your list can easily become a thorn in your side and a persistent drain on your motivation. The key to maximizing your productivity lies in keeping your list short, relevant and realistic.

2 DO

This is at the heart of every to-do list and constitutes those things in which we will invest the time, effort and energy to ensure they are completed. Thus it is crucial that **only tasks which really must be actioned** are kept here – and every single task in this list must truly earn and deserve its place. The other side of the coin is that **everything on this list must be completed,** and as quickly as possible.

3 DELAY

If used appropriately, this category can prove extremely valuable. If misused, it will be a permanent stumbling block. By ensuring that you review and revise your list frequently, and that you are realistic and ruthless with your decisions about which tasks will stay on your list and in which category, it will serve as a very useful repository, ensuring that nothing gets forgotten or left undone. If it is allowed to become simply a dumping ground with the misguided notion that getting tasks down on paper gets them out of your head and is therefore somehow halfway to getting them done, then it is very likely to hold you back and actively get in the way of completing tasks, slowing you down and impairing your productivity.

 Remember this: Complete or delete!

Productive organization and prioritization

We have seen how important it is to be realistic and ruthless when compiling and sorting your list in order for that list to be meaningful and genuinely useful. It is just as important, however, that you are rigorous in your organization of the list, ensuring that items are both categorized and prioritized. The easiest way to do this is in two stages:

STAGE 1

1 **Describe** – What exactly is the task?

2 **Deduce** – How important is it? How relevant is it? Should it be deleted, done or delayed?

3 **Decide** – What priority should the task be given?

4 **Discard** – Once the task is on the list and in the correct place, it can be removed from wherever it was previously stored.

STAGE 2

▶ **Anything which you decide can be deleted from the list should be done so straightaway.** Purging your list regularly is a great way to keep it simple and uncluttered so that you can see at a glance what needs to get done and by when. It also has the considerable benefit of ensuring that you feel on top of the situation and in control – and that things are getting done and you're making progress.

▶ **Anything which you decide can be done should be attributed the appropriate priority so that there is a clear and definite order.** By deciding on a sequence at this stage, you don't need to look through your list each time you revisit it – simply work from the top down and things will be completed in the correct order.

▶ **Anything which you decide can be delayed should be attributed the appropriate priority so that you can see at a glance which task is the next to be elevated to the 'Do' category.** This might be because room becomes available on the list by other items being completed and removed, or because the task itself assumes a higher priority (e.g. alteration of project circumstances or a change in your needs). Alternatively, it may become possible to delete items so you should get into the habit of going through this list on a regular basis.

Increasing your flexibility

> 'A self does not amount to much, but no self is an island; each exists in a fabric of relations that is now more complex and mobile than ever before.'
>
> Jean-François Lyotard

Increasing your flexibility to meet the day-to-day demands of your work and to ensure that every minute is spent in the most productive way possible is key to maximizing your productivity. In order to focus exclusively on one piece of work, the best approach is to temporarily deny yourself access to all means of communication and thus deny other people access to you. However, when you need to open the channels of communication you need to make sure that you do so with maximum efficiency.

Indeed, for some people the option to be 'offline' simply does not exist, so the channels of communication must always be open (e.g. if you need to stay in constant contact with suppliers, or to ensure your clients have instant access to you no matter where you are). Businesses are catering for an increasingly demanding consumer base for whom deadlines are tighter and expectations higher, driven by the growth of a service-based economy, and thus there has never been greater pressure to respond quickly to clients, to access information immediately, and to maintain communication continually.

And for those people who do have a choice, sometimes the best option is to be 'online' anyway. This is because sitting at a desk day after day doing the same work takes its toll, and if you feel that you have become stuck in a rut and need to shake up your routine in order to re-energize yourself then one great way to boost your productivity is to take advantage of today's communication technology to free yourself from the office and spend some time working in another location. They say that a change is as good as a rest and sometimes a new perspective and change of environment is exactly what is required to give your productivity a much-needed boost.

Fortunately, in today's world of fast-paced high-tech information superhighways it is perfectly possible to work anywhere you please, in any number of ways which suit you because today's office packs up and fits neatly into a small holdall. Armed with a smart phone, a tablet computer or wireless connectivity laptop, and a 3G dongle or personal hotspot capability we can go where the wind blows us, where we need to be or where we want to be. Indeed, for many people it makes little business sense to operate from a single office but rather to do business on the move to make the best use of their time and resources, and this peripatetic style of working is a growing trend.

'Management Futures', a report from the Chartered Management Institute (CMI) concluded that developments in mobile working technology will increasingly enable the rise of 'virtual businesses' so that by 2018 a good deal of business will be completed through virtual contact alone, with efficient project management and the ability to work effectively from home two of the key skills workers will need to master. So, while open channels of communication, if not carefully managed, can be a significant barrier to productivity, equally they can help to give it a much-needed boost. The key is to rigorously audit your needs and the needs of your situation in order to find the most productive way of utilizing communication technologies for your situation.

Shaking up your routine

If you need inspiration and your creative batteries are running low, or if you simply need a change of scene, being able to pack your office into your briefcase and leave your usual office space behind can provide a welcome relief and a much-needed breath of fresh air – quite literally, if you so choose. By supercharging your ability to function you will be boosting your ability to be productive, with the added benefit that the results will be almost immediate.

Case study

'I have a favourite coffee shop in town. This is a place I can escape to whenever I feel the need for a change of scene, somewhere I can go to write or think and as they have Wi-Fi there it makes working there easy. There are times at which I feel my productivity running lower and lower and then I know it's time for a coffee escape!'

Certainly, many people find that one of the best 'quick fix' solutions to boosting their productivity is to throw everything they need into a bag and head off to a local coffee shop. This is particularly useful whenever you want to gain some perspective on a situation and where physically getting away from the office really helps, or when motivation is waning and just having other people around and being 'in public' will spur you on; or on a beautiful summer's day you might opt to swap the bag for a set of panniers and jump on a bicycle to combine work with exercise, a change of scene and a liberal dose of uplifting sunshine and fresh air. Of course, this isn't always possible but, when it is, making use of it is a great way to blow away the cobwebs and shake up your routine, providing some much-needed stimulus for your productivity.

Remember this: Take advantage of mobile working

Research has shown that 57 per cent of businesses offer mobile working to their employees in order to improve their work/life balance, which in turn ensures that their staff members are as motivated and productive as possible. If you are free to take advantage of this flexibility, then make the most of the productivity stimulus afforded by mobile working. If you are not, try to find alternatives – or to introduce this concept in your workplace.

The ability to shake up your routine in this way also makes working more enjoyable, but the crucial aspect is that it has been proven to increase business productivity. A survey from the Department of Business Enterprise and Regulatory Reform (BERR) found that 65 per cent of companies think that a flexible working routine improves staff motivation, with 50 per cent reporting increased productivity as a result. So if you feel like you need a change of scene, then in all probability you really will benefit from the change, and so will your work.

Being ever ready

So how does mobile working actually work, and can you employ it in your work life to help maximize your productivity? No matter where you are, no matter where you are going, getting set up with the right equipment allows you to always be 'at the office'. This can be a great advantage for your clients, knowing that they can always reach you, and providing an uninterrupted service in this way not only exudes efficiency and professionalism but boosts your ability to be productive.

Furthermore, they will be reassured that, when they do contact you, you will be ready and able to converse on whatever it is they need to discuss since you will always have everything to hand. Just be careful to ensure that any time you have overtly ringfenced is appropriately safeguarded.

With no downtime, since you are always ready to work, it's a great way to maximize your productivity. Perhaps your clients want to arrange a meeting or conference call, discuss a piece of research you sent them or walk you through a PowerPoint presentation they have just sent you as an attachment to an email – whatever it is, you will be able to get to it in a matter of minutes and your clients will be reassured knowing that you are always on hand to help them.

Remember this: Productivity inspires confidence

Not only is it important for you to be as productive as possible at all times and in all things but it is also important to convey this image to your clients, customers and colleagues. Knowing that you are 100-percent productive is a great way to inspire confidence in them and to showcase your abilities.

Your complete portfolio

How many times have you gone to a meeting assuming you were fully prepared only to discover that the client is also very interested in a completely different area, one which you deal with but not one for which you have resource material to hand? Of course, you could always try to explain what it is you do and how you might be able to help them and you can promise faithfully to send them some examples as soon as you get back to the office, but you will already have missed that golden moment, the one which offers you the very best opportunity to impress.

Productivity in this sense is not only a case of how much you can achieve but also how much you are able to gain through that achievement. How much better is it to be able to show your client precisely what it is you can do, right there and then, by showing them examples of similar projects you have already completed for other clients?

> 'If you are prepared, you will be confident, and will do the job.'
>
> Tom Landry

Not only does mobile working allow you to seize the initiative, it ensures you can walk a client through your offer, explaining it to them first-hand and answering their questions. It also shows just how efficient and prepared you are, thereby giving your clients, or prospective clients, confidence in your work and your working practices. This not only makes you more productive in your work, it also makes you more productive in the way you get future work.

Turning dead time into work time

A significant barrier to productivity is finding yourself confronted with dead time, time which could have been used productively had you been adequately prepared. Instead, you have no option but to watch the clock tick by, the time and opportunity wasted. Finding yourself with time to kill but not being able to use it efficiently is one of the great frustrations with modern working practices. It is a situation which occurs all too often: while waiting for a meeting to start (you left extra early to give yourself plenty of time only for there to have been no traffic and now you have arrived at your destination with time to kill); at the airport waiting for your delayed flight to be called; in a soulless hotel room where some interesting work would prove a timely distraction, and so on. And each and every wasted opportunity is not just a barrier to your productivity – it cuts it stone dead.

There can surely be no greater impediment to your productivity than time which is spent doing nothing, and knowing that this is time which could have been used constructively can be soul-destroying. Remember that anything which seems to you to be a waste of time is therefore wasted time, and that is something you simply cannot afford if you are seeking to maximize your productivity.

'I do not want to waste any time. And if you are not working on important things, you are wasting time.'

Dean Kamen

Fortunately, by getting organized and setting yourself up with an efficient mobile working suite the horrors of dead time can be not just minimized but eliminated altogether. The trick is to get into good habits – always make sure you take everything with you, all the time, wherever you go and for however long, whether or not you think there will be any need for them, or even if you absolutely know for certain that there won't be. That way, when the unexpected or even inconceivable happens and you find yourself with time to kill you will be ready to take advantage of it.

Getting organized

Getting yourself set up with a fully flexible working arrangement which is perfectly suited to you and your needs will require some careful consideration and perhaps also some not inconsiderable upfront costs. However, it is an investment which can pay for itself in a very short space of time.

If you want to keep yourself well organized and efficient (and why wouldn't you? – after all, these attributes are key to maximizing your productivity), then you will need someone or something to organize your diary and field your calls. Unless you are fortunate enough to have a personal assistant, taking advantage of today's technology to help you handle the tasks yourself will most likely be your best option.

After all, you need only ever be a phone call or voicemail away and you will always have your diary with you. Need to book a flight or a venue for a meeting? No problem. At your fingertips you have the single best resource available to anyone, the World Wide Web, and you have the wherewithal to book whatever you need to book, and with some dextrous time management you can ensure you are filling one of those dread spots of otherwise dead time we have already looked at, so it shouldn't even cause you unnecessary delay.

An efficient setup such as this can also help with revenue generation. If by having an efficient mobile working setup you can win work you might otherwise have lost out on, then that surely is the ultimate in workplace productivity!

Travel time

A barrier to productivity which can be hard to avoid but which must be carefully managed is time spent travelling. Of course, as we have already seen, if you can utilize this time to complete some work then the time spent travelling need not be wasted. However, this applies only to the time actually spent in transit, and only if this time really can be utilized. As any frequent traveller knows, a large proportion of travelling time consists of getting in and out of vehicles, walking while heavily laden, checking in and going through customs, security checks, etc. This portion of your time cannot reasonably be utilized in any practical way to further your work. It stands to reason, then, that the more you can limit your need to travel the more productive you can be.

Exactly how you manage this will depend on your situation and the needs of your work, but studies have shown that a large number of business trips undertaken every year are in fact not necessary. Could the meeting you are going to be combined with another meeting at a later date? Could it be achieved just as effectively with a teleconference or video conference, thus saving you the need to travel in person? Would sending material, either physically or electronically, to be read and digested in advance, reduce the need to travel or even eliminate it altogether?

If you really do need to travel (e.g. to attend a meeting, meet a client or present some work in person), then consider the possibility that your meeting could be combined with another meeting with a different client or colleague in the same town or country. If you can effect two meetings with the same piece of travel, rather than having to travel twice to attend the two meetings separately, then you are in effect halving your travel time – and doubling your productivity in the process. In the quest to maximize your productivity, the amount of time you spend travelling, and therefore the amount of dead time in your work life, needs to be carefully thought through and managed – and where possible avoided.

Effective time/work management

Effective time/work management is an extremely important aspect of maximizing your productivity and one which is becoming more and more important with modern work practices, particularly as information and communication technologies continue to get better, faster and more efficient. One of the basic tenets of time/work management, and one which will very directly affect your ability to be productive, is to try to ensure that you tackle several jobs of a roughly similar nature in one go, before moving on to another group of similar jobs, and so on.

As we saw earlier in this chapter, a lot of time is wasted by flitting from one type of task to another, and then to another and another, as there is always a transition period required which is inevitably just dead time. Different pieces of equipment (hardware or software) may need to be removed and others put in their place; you will need to make the mental transition from one sort of task to another (often accompanied by a 'much-needed' break for a transitional cup of tea or coffee); information and documents may need to be located and relevant people contacted (e.g. accountant, legal adviser, suppliers or clients) so that you can establish pertinent facts and so forth.

And with each transition comes a loss of productivity. This is especially true of small tasks where the transition period can often equal, and sometimes even outweigh, the length of time required to complete the tasks themselves. Thus it follows that, if you can get all your ducks in a row to begin with, you can save yourself a lot of wasted time and effort and a good deal of needless frustration.

Remember this: Be disciplined

Maximizing workplace efficiency through disciplined organization is vital to maximizing workplace productivity.

The best way to go about this is to identify which tasks can readily be combined into groups of a similar nature, and how often such tasks need to be completed, which can wait and which are urgent, and so on. Then identify the optimal number of tasks which can be completed in one session. Obviously, this will depend on the nature and type of each task or group of tasks, and it is likely that no two groups will be exactly the same, so try to establish the rules for each group individually. By knowing the length of time required to complete each task and the frequency at which the tasks occur you can plan ahead to ensure they are completed in a timely manner. Moreover, by sorting tasks into relevant work groups you will ensure they are completed in manageable sections, not piecemeal or randomly, making them easier to deal with as well as allowing you to approach them more efficiently.

> 'The highest type of efficiency is that which can utilize existing material to the best advantage.'
>
> Jawaharlal Nehru

So capitalize on the flexibility provided by mobile working to ensure that, no matter where you are and regardless of the project or projects on which you are currently employed, you have to hand every single piece of work you need to complete so that you can always work on a logical group of work pieces in one go. By eliminating the need to cherry-pick your work and the sequence in which it is completed, you will streamline your working practices, thus making you more efficient and more effective, and increasing your productivity substantially with very little extra effort required on your part.

Next step

In this chapter we have looked at how to maximize your productivity by organizing and prioritizing tasks as well as using modern working practices such as mobile working to your advantage. In the next chapter we will look at how you can set some basic rules and boundaries for yourself that will keep you focused, alert and fulfilled.

4

Setting Limits

In this chapter you will learn how to:

▶ *Trim down your work processes and structures and increase their effectiveness – and your productivity*

▶ *Get rid of unwanted stress; some stress in your work life can be a good thing: but too much can quickly become detrimental to your productivity*

▶ *Ensure your work is giving you what you need – if your work is taking more than it is giving, then there is an unhealthy imbalance which must be corrected*

▶ *Only take on work which is appropriate and don't be tempted to take on too much.*

How do you feel?

1 Do you have sufficient time to complete the work you undertake?

2 Are your work processes lean and effective?

3 Does your work create unwanted stress?

4 Is your focus in the right place? Is your work life giving you pleasure and energy or draining you?

5 Do you take on too much work? Is the work you accept always appropriate?

25 hours a day, 8 days a week

Imagine that you could create a twenty-fifth hour in every day, or better still an eighth day in every week. And imagine that that day was devoted exclusively to the needs of your work life. Suddenly, you would have enough time to get done everything you need to do, the quality of your work would improve as you could afford the extra time necessary to fine-tune and polish your output, and your stress levels would plummet as you would replace clock-watching and the dread of looming deadlines with a measured and relaxed approach to your work. You might even begin to enjoy your work in a way previously unimaginable.

This may sound like a workplace dream but it is entirely possible to achieve this lifestyle, mental wellbeing, and improved work output within the constraints of your current working life simply by following some basic rules. And if you currently work all hours and weekends, too, then you will quickly discover that by implementing these structures you begin to get back some of the leisure time work has stolen from you – maybe all of it!

Remember this: Double your productivity

If you can double your productivity, then you will effectively double your capacity. Achieving twice as much in the same space of time and with the same resources is possible through implementing a robust system to boost your productivity.

No matter how hard we work and no matter how productive we are, our capacity for production, whatever our work involves, is finite. While learning to be more productive means you can get more done in the same number of hours, there will still be a limit to what can be achieved. So, rather than letting these limits define what you do, make this decision for yourself and set your own limits around what it is you have decided to do.

By taking on as many projects as is feasibly possible in the hope that the *quantity* of the work you produce will be sufficient to impress, you are automatically restricting what can be put into those projects. In other words, you have chosen to go for quantity rather than quality. This scattergun approach – hoping that, if you do enough work, at least some of it will be decent – is a sure-fire recipe for mediocrity. It is far better to set realistic limits as to what can be meaningfully achieved and concentrate on these, ensuring that the work you are producing is of the highest quality. In order to do this, you will need to analyse each piece of work which comes your way to decide whether or not it is something you should be taking on. This simple table will help you to do just that:

Work offered	How long will it take to complete?	How much energy will it require?	What other resources will it demand?	What's in it for me?

If the last box seems rather selfish, that's because it is – and it absolutely should be. If you work for a large company, then it stands to reason that there's something in it for the company, so the question you need to ask yourself is what is in it for you. If you work for yourself, then you *are* the company, so the question remains the same. If you are to maximize your productivity, then there is simply no room for taking on work which doesn't take you where you want to go.

A good analogy for this is the side-by-side comparison of two artists. They are equally skilled and identically equipped – in other words, there is nothing to separate them other than their approach to productivity. And they both have the same desires – fame and money! One of them decides that the best way to make his fortune and his reputation is to paint as much as he possibly can. The volume of work he produces is considerable as he churns out 30 paintings every month. Each of his paintings, however, is of limited quality and each therefore fetches a low price while he establishes himself as a mediocre artist.

His competitor takes the opposite approach. He decides that it is better to concentrate on producing just one painting and ensuring that it is superb. It takes him the entire month but his creation is a masterpiece, making him considerably more money from his one painting then his competitor realized from all 30 of his. In addition, he quickly establishes a reputation for quality. This means that as the years go by he is able to charge more and more for his work as people are convinced by his ability and want to invest in him. His competitor, on the other hand, has backed himself into a corner and can only charge the minimum amount for each of his paintings, never able to up his price. And all the while he is constantly straining to achieve the high volume of work he must produce in order to earn a living, making himself tired and stressed in the process and realizing very little in the way of job satisfaction, while the more successful artist is relaxed, calm and thoroughly enjoying his work and his situation.

So it is better to take on less work and focus on the quality of your output. Be careful, however, not to use this as a ready-made excuse for not taking on as much work as you are capable of doing and doing well. The key to maximizing your productivity is in being selective about the work you take on and learning not to just accept everything people try to put your way, and ensuring that the work you do accept you do brilliantly.

Remember this: More or less?
If less is more, just think how much more more could be!

Quality not quantity

Have you ever tried your hand at copywriting? If not, give it a go. It is a great way to see how setting limits can improve the quality of your output. Since 'copy' is simply text, then you are in effect writing copy every time you write an email. The time you spend on the composition, however, is likely to be fairly minimal. If you need to write a piece of text for a client document, on the other hand, you are likely to spend more time on it, honing it, polishing it and improving it.

Now imagine that the text, or 'copy', is 200 words long and that you are presented with the challenge of reducing this to 150 words. You need to keep all of the essential information but must find a way to convey it more succinctly. What happens when you do this is that you get rid of all the words which don't need to be there but were simply adding bulk and therefore diluting your message.

Now imagine that you have to reduce your text still further, down to just 100 words. At first, this may seem impossible without losing some of the information but with practice you will find that it is perfectly possible. In order to achieve it, however, a radical rethink is required. You can no longer simply rely on paring down what you had already written. Instead, you will need to adopt a fresh approach, finding ways to rewrite your copy in order to present your ideas in the most succinct manner possible. And what happens when you do this is that your work improves in a number of ways:

▶ Because it is shorter, it is more likely to be read.

▶ Because it is more succinct, it will be more memorable.

▶ Because you have had to choose your words with such care, your sentences will have more impact.

▶ Because you have pared your copy down to the bare essentials, your readership will approach it in a different way.

This last point is an interesting one as it often occurs at a subconscious level, but typically your readers will concentrate harder on taking in your words since they know that, because there is no padding, every word is important and must be taken on board. So, whatever your line of work, try to take the copywriter's approach. Strip back what you are doing to the bare essentials to make it powerful and memorable – and don't fall into the trap of thinking that productivity is measured in the volume of your output.

Remember this: Quality, not quantity

Focus on quality, not quantity. Remember that if you don't really have anything to add to a project, discussion, email conversation, etc., then it is better to say nothing. Interjections of no consequence and waffle are a waste of your time and a waste of everyone else's time.

Quick fix: Add value, not volume

Try thinking through a typical day at work. How many times do you have the opportunity to add an opinion, comment or suggestion to a conversation, project, etc. And how many times do you do so? Then be honest with yourself and think about how many of these are really valuable and how many are just adding volume, not value. Try to keep this in the back of your mind and use it as a handy filter to help you to know when to add something and when not to.

By getting into the habit of doing this with all your work it will become second nature and you will quickly find that as a result four things occur, all of which are fundamental to boosting your productivity:

1 Tasks are completely more quickly.

2 The output of the tasks is more impactful.

3 People prioritize your output because:

   ▷ it is quicker to read

   ▷ it is lean and direct

   ▷ it only occurs when you really have something to say.

4 You have more time for other tasks.

And the best part of it is that they will happen automatically as a by-product of your approach, requiring no thought or effort from you other than to decide when to provide input and when not to.

Remember this

Limiting what you take on does not limit what you can achieve.

Determining your priorities

While it may be possible to be working on several things at once, you should never have more than one thing as your priority if you are to achieve maximum productivity. It is therefore crucial that you determine your priority at any given time and you will need to allow flexibility in your working to allow your priority to change according to your needs. It may be that you have one clear priority for the week ahead but a different priority for today, and that the priority for the next hour is something different again. The trick is to ensure that you know what needs to be the centre of your focus, for how long, and why, and that you always keep in mind the bigger picture so that your temporary priorities do not steal time from your long-term priority. Given the speed and complexity of today's working practices, having this sort of flexibility is crucial to achieve maximum productivity.

Remember this: One priority at a time

Although you may have different priorities over the course of a week, or even a day, only one will ever be your priority at any one time. If it feels as though there are two or more tasks which are equally important and urgent, you will need to determine other qualities which make one your priority – then focus on that one alone.

Streamlining

It has been said that creating to-do lists is a great way of ensuring that nothing ever gets done! The truth is that with the demands of modern working you can all too easily find yourself creating a to-do list at the beginning of the day which you then diligently arrange in order of priorities, all of which will have changed by mid-morning and the majority of which are completely irrelevant by lunchtime. Simply creating to-do lists and structuring them is clearly insufficient to meeting the demands of today's working practices. What is needed is the ability to streamline.

HOW STREAMLINING WORKS

Imagine a yacht sailing through choppy waters. As the sea conditions worsen and more and more is thrown at it, and with greater and greater force, the boat is forced to slow because it is unable to glide over the water and waves crash down upon it. It will pitch and roll and the crew will have to fight harder and harder to keep it moving in the right direction. As the winds worsen they may be forced to take down the sails to prevent the ship capsizing. Eventually, they may come to a complete standstill, at the mercy of the elements and no longer able to effect any control.

All too often this is what it is like for us in our working lives as the volume and urgency of additional and often unforeseen work slows us further and further, threatening to overturn us completely, until we come to a complete standstill. Our inability to streamline has reduced our productivity to zero.

Now imagine a submarine navigating the same waters. It glides through them impervious to all that is happening above the water, its progress unimpeded and its crew unstressed. Raising the periscope will give the captain sight of what is happening above the water, so he is not oblivious, but he remains entirely calm and in control and, crucially, progressing at a steady rate and in the right direction. And because the captain is not allowing his submarine to be affected by external elements his vessel's productivity never dips below 100 per cent.

This is streamlining. If the captain were to take the submarine above the waterline, it would soon become impeded – but not to the same extent as the yacht. This is for two reasons:

1 It has its own power source.

2 It is streamlined, free of sails, masts, etc.

So it must be in your work. Having a clear focus provides the necessary drive (power) and having only one frees you from additional trappings which can slow you.

Implementing streamlining in your work life

In order to be streamlined in your working practices you need to ensure that you:

▶ have a **clear focus**

▶ **limit** your focus to only **one** thing

- **understand** exactly what you are trying to **achieve**
- know **how** you will accomplish it
- do not allow yourself to be **sidetracked**
- do not allow yourself to be **distracted.**

By deciding your priority and thinking through what the task entails and what would constitute a good result, you can accomplish the first four of these points relatively easily. The last two, however, can be much more difficult to implement.

NOT ALLOWING YOURSELF TO BE SIDETRACKED OR DISTRACTED

While you can't, and indeed shouldn't, be oblivious to additional needs and pressures in your work life as they occur, neither should you allow yourself to be distracted by them, or for them to pull focus. Allowing yourself to be sidetracked every time a new situation occurs is a quick route to achieving precious little.

Responding to emails as they occur, for instance, is a pitfall which must be avoided since it prevents you from streamlining. For starters, the emails will inevitably cover a range of different topics forcing you to switch mentally back and forth in order to compose a useful reply. This takes both time and energy, but what is even worse is that each one creates a little more stress in your day. By getting into the habit of streamlining how you deal with your emails, you can all but eradicate this stress while freeing up more time and ensuring your responses are focused and useful.

So let's take this as an example to see how implementing the technique of streamlining can help you to maximize your productivity – and what happens if you *don't* streamline. Let's suppose that you have a job in which during the course of a typical day you might receive dozens of emails from a number of different people and that these might cover a range of topics, projects and tasks. Not streamlining your approach for dealing with them means that you will be distracted every few minutes throughout the day as your attention, focus and energy are pulled in all directions, and your productivity decreases sharply. Streamlining, on the other hand, will allow you to stay in control of your workflow and achieve more with less effort and less stress.

STREAMLINING

Emails are one of the biggest bugbears in modern work life and can easily turn from an annoying distraction to a productivity-crippling interruption. It is therefore vitally important that they be dealt with appropriately – and that no matter how odd it might seem at first you are very strict with yourself in implementing the most appropriate way of dealing with them for your situation.

▶ **If possible, disable emails.** Quite simply the best way to ensure you are not distracted by answering unwanted emails is to not see them in the first place! Of course, they will need to be dealt with eventually but **it is much more efficient to deal with them en masse than to answer them piecemeal.** So if your job allows for this, then simply cut away from your emails while you complete the task at hand and then open your emails at a time of your choosing and deal with them. In this way, answering your emails is not a nuisance interruption to the task at hand but rather it *becomes* the task at hand and therefore can be dealt with just as productively as any other task.

▶ If this is not possible, perhaps because some emails will need to be acknowledged as they arrive, then it is important to get into the habit of merely glancing at the emails to **see whether or not they require an acknowledgement, acknowledging those that do, and moving on.** Do not be tempted to actually *deal* with the emails. This should be left until later when dealing with your emails will be your number-one priority and can take all of your focus.

▶ In the worst-case scenario (and unfortunately many unenlightened bosses make this all too common), **there may be some communications with which you are expected to deal as and when they occur.** In this situation the approach is really no different except that you must determine those emails which really *must* be dealt with immediately and simply cannot be deferred, so that it is these, and only these, which you deal with as you go along.

For all other emails you follow the steps outlined above.

NOT STREAMLINING

▶ You **do not disable** emails.

▶ As they pour in throughout the day **you deal with them one by one.**

▶ Each time you do so:

  ▷ it **breaks your focus from the job in hand** (the one you had previously identified as your priority and which should be the recipient of all your focus);

  ▷ it forces you to make the **mental shift** to whatever the new email concerns;

  ▷ it **takes time** to make the transition as well as potentially impairing the quality of the work which is your main focus;

  ▷ you may have to refer to something (or someone) else in order to draft a response, **costing you further time;**

  ▷ you are on **tenterhooks** waiting for the next email which will disturb you;

  ▷ you get back to the task at hand and **waste further time** remembering where you had got up to and getting back up to speed.

So you can see just how damaging not streamlining your working practices can be; and while you can work around it if you have no choice but to monitor all your emails as and when they arrive, it is far better to disable them in the first place and remove the problem.

Remember this

'Prevention is better than cure.'

Quick fix: Disable your email for short periods

Even if it isn't possible to turn off your emails for an entire day, it may well be possible to disable them for short periods. Even knowing just that you won't be disturbed for the next hour or two can greatly boost your productivity.

Dealing with work life stress

For most of us work can certainly be stressful at times, and, while this cannot be altogether avoided, it can be dealt with appropriately in order to minimize the negative effects of its interruption. At its worst, stress can be destructive both for your work and your health. Positive stress, on the other hand, when harnessed and used correctly can help you to be more productive by giving you more energy and a greater impetus to succeed.

Perhaps a better term for positive stress, then, is 'positive pressure', and interestingly the differences between damaging stress and positive pressure largely boil down to one thing: damaging stress is almost always a result of *external factors* – for example, the expectations of our colleagues, bosses or clients (which can often be unreasonable or unrealistic) or arbitrary timescales imposed on us.

Positive pressure is the opposite as it comes from *within* – it is the pressure we put on ourselves; pressure to succeed, pressure to win, pressure to do our best. And because we are in control of this pressure we can manage it appropriately and harness its ability to impel us toward achieving our goals, ensuring that it never crosses the line into becoming damaging stress.

Positive pressure	Damaging stress
▶ imposed on us by ourselves	▶ imposed on us by others
▶ helpful	▶ unhelpful
▶ within our control	▶ outside of our control
▶ empowering	▶ limiting
▶ can be turned on and off as necessary	▶ permanent and persistent
▶ caused by excitement and anticipation	▶ caused by worry and fear

Positive pressure, then, can be seen as a *resource* which can be tapped into at will and as such can enable us to boost our productivity. Negative stress, on the other hand, can be seen as a *barrier* to productivity and as such must be staunchly avoided. By setting limits to what we take on, and by determining before we begin what a good result will comprise (so that we can easily recognize it when we get there and not keep beating ourselves up, putting in 50 per cent more work to improve the output by 1 per cent), we can generate for ourselves the degree of positive pressure which is most useful for us, and eliminate any negative stress.

Disrupting interruptions

One of the most common causes of workplace stress and anxiety, and one of the biggest barriers to productivity, is the incessant stream of interruptions to which most people are subjected every day in their work lives. We have looked at emails but these are only one source of potential interruptions – others include:

▶ phone calls

▶ instant messages

▶ social media

▶ face-to-face interruptions

- video calls
- texts.

If we are not careful to regulate them, these can negatively impact our productivity in a number of ways:

- **Wasting time**
  - How many of these communications really are essential?
  - How many really cannot wait and have to be dealt with right now?

- **Breaking focus**
  - Constant distractions make it very easy to lose your train of thought, or to lose a good idea – sometimes permanently.
  - Any momentum built up is quickly and easily lost.

- **Flitting between tasks**
  - Every time we leave a task to deal with a new communication we are having to spend time mentally adjusting to the new requirements, and then mentally readjusting to the original task.

The ease with which we can communicate today and the immediacy with which it happens can be a blessing but it can also be a curse – and unless carefully managed it is more likely to be the latter! If you not able to restrict others' access to you through these channels but you are in a position to keep the lines of communication open but limit the frequency with which they are used and to determine the channels available, then this will very likely be your best option. In this case, although it might seem somewhat extreme, you will have to adopt an all-or-nothing approach. The easiest and most efficient way to effect this is, as we have seen, to close the lines of communication between certain times. But does this really work? And how can it best be managed?

By switching off your Internet connection so that you cannot be emailed or messaged, and by switching off your mobile phone and/or landline, together with disciplining yourself not to check any social networking sites, you will be:

- safeguarding yourself from interruptions
- ring-fencing your time
- protecting your focus
- preventing your energy from being depleted
- ensuring that your productivity cannot be inadvertently damaged by others.

Clearly it is impractical for most people to become a complete recluse (however tempting it might be at times!), so the simplest solution is to open the channels of communication at certain times, for instance between 5 p.m. and 6.30 p.m. If you work in a shared office environment, interruptions may also come from well-meaning colleagues, which can be more difficult to prevent. However, by putting the word out that for the next couple of hours you should not be disturbed, unless it is a genuine emergency, you should be able to safeguard a block of time in which you can focus, and by devoting all your energy to one project during this uninterrupted time you will maximize your productivity.

Focusing on those things which give you pleasure and energy

In order to maximize your productivity you will need to be selective in what you do and learn to concentrate your efforts on just a few things which you can then do brilliantly. A powerful technique to help you to decide where you should focus your time and energy revolves around seeing where these are currently focused and determining whether these are the areas which are most profitable for you. If they are not, you will need to work out:

- what are the areas to which your time and energy should be devoted

- ► why your efforts are currently centred in the wrong place

- ► what you will need to do to focus them more productively

- ► whether your work life is giving you what you need.
  If not:

  - ▷ Can this be remedied within your current work situation?

  - ▷ Is it time for a more fundamental change in your work life? If so, what?

It is a process much favoured by life coaches since it helps their clients to determine what they should and shouldn't be spending their resources on in their work lives, and also in their home lives. Far too often, when we realize we are not being as productive as we could – and should – be, we employ the Victorian workplace mentality of simply putting our heads down and pushing on, grinding our way through the barriers. It is much better, however, to lift your head and take a good, long, honest look at your situation. It may be that you only need to implement some subtle changes in your work life, or your work life/home life balance, to achieve the desired result. On the other hand, it may be that some fundamental changes are required in order to remedy the situation. Whichever it is, the one universal truth is that only by understanding the situation and its challenges can you overcome them. In this case, knowledge really is power.

Try it now: Check your work/life balance

It is possible to get the right work/life balance and still pay the mortgage! To see whether or not you have got the balance right, draw a pie chart and divide it according to those things which are currently taking your time and energy – the more they're taking the bigger the slice of pie. Then draw another pie chart and divide it according to those things which give you energy and pleasure. Then compare the two. If you discover that your work has a greater prominence in the first chart than in the second, then the balance is awry and you will need to work to redress this as quickly as possible.

Flexibility and fluidity

Clearly, there is a need to capture all the tasks which need to be accomplished, and within a specified timeframe, but if to-do lists, calendars and diaries are to have relevance in today's frenetic business world, then we need to effect a major shift in our approach to using them – and this requires flexibility and fluidity. Simply put, we need to have the ability to introduce flexibility and fluidity into our structured work lives so that we can adapt to situations as they change without ever losing our grip on the bigger picture.

Imagine that you are standing in a relaxed pose with your feet facing forward and shoulder width apart, your knees slightly bent, and that someone stands in front of you and pushes your left shoulder. What happens? Your left shoulder moves backward and, instantly, with no thought or effort on your part, your hips rotate to accommodate the force, your left leg straightens slightly while your right knee dips, and your right shoulder moves forward to accommodate the force. And all the while your feet remain firmly planted and facing forward, quietly untroubled. In other words, your body has soaked up the force of the new input and immediately dealt with it in such a way as to stabilize you. Establishing this firm platform enables you to deal with any new pressures without ever being knocked off balance or forced to take a backward step.

So it must be with your work. As things occur, often out of the blue, you must be able to deal with them immediately without being pushed off balance and without your central focus being disturbed. In the same way that it is the flexibility and fluidity of the posture which allows for this, so it is the flexibility and fluidity of the structure we build for our work which will allow it to accommodate the unexpected. It must be firm but not rigid, stout but not unyielding, a secure base securing a flexible and fluid structure. In this way unexpected events which could otherwise have thrown us off course are easily absorbed and dealt with, and we retain the ability to stay heading in the right direction.

IS WHAT YOU'RE DOING WHAT YOU *SHOULD* BE DOING?

Since you can only realistically do one thing at a time if you are to do it to the best of your ability, it is crucial that you ensure that whatever you're doing is what you should be doing. Ask yourself:

▶ Is this my **highest-priority** task?

▶ Is this the task which **most urgently** requires my attention?

▶ Is this the task which I am **best set up** to be tackling?

▶ Is this what I should be doing **right now**?

If the answer to any of those questions is 'no', then you will need to either adjust your situation to fit the task or, in most cases, adjust the task to fit your situation:

ADJUSTING YOUR SITUATION TO FIT THE TASK

If you have identified that this is indeed the piece of work on which you should be concentrating, but that you are not properly set up to tackle it, you will need to adjust your situation to fit the task. Do you have all the information you require? Are you physically in the right place to complete the task? Are you mentally in the right place to complete the task? Do you need to get someone's permission, opinion, buy-in, etc. before you can complete, or even begin, the task? Whatever it is that is holding you back must be identified and rectified so that you can concentrate on precisely what you should be doing, and do it with maximum productivity.

ADJUSTING THE TASK TO FIT YOUR SITUATION

It is true for most people that there are certain pieces of work we enjoy tackling more than others and it is these to which we most willingly devote our time and energy. It stands to reason – after all, it is human nature to put off and put off anything we're really not looking forward to doing. This is why it is so important to dispassionately identify your most urgent priority and to concentrate on that, adopting the task which needs to be completed rather than one you will most enjoy tackling.

Productive focus

One of the key tenets to improving your productivity is learning how to pare things down to the essential and focusing only on that. It is a commonly held belief (though often it is held subconsciously) that the more we do, the more we take on, the busier we are and the busier we are seen to be, the more productive we are, and the more productive we appear to be. In truth, however, real productivity lies in getting things done, not in simply taking them on. And while undertaking numerous projects may make us seem busy, it will all too quickly become evident that we are simply busy fighting to stay afloat, and that we are actually achieving very little. To be truly productive, you should take on only the amount of work you can reasonably expect to be able to do to the best of your ability. With each piece of work you do accept you must:

- set rigid **limits** and stick to them
- pare the work down to the **bare essentials**
- define and identify what are **unnecessary trappings** and strip them away
- **simplify** the task
- focus on the **most important** elements
- gets these done **quickly** and **efficiently** and move on.

> **Remember this:** Limit your volume of work
>
> By strictly limiting the volume of work you take on you will make it easier to clarify where you should concentrate your focus. You will also free yourself up to achieve maximum productivity through channelling all your resources on one task at a time.

Learning to say 'no'

One of the best ways to ensure that you achieve everything you take on is to make sure that you don't take on too much in the first place. This may sound like obvious advice but it is amazing how rarely it is followed in the workplace. This is often because of one of two key reasons:

1 We are put under pressure from **our bosses or colleagues** to take on more and more work.

2 We put **ourselves** under pressure to take on more and more work.

Ironically, it is the first of these which is often the easiest to deal with. If you feel that your productivity is suffering because you have more work than you can reasonably handle, then the answer might be as simple as communicating this to those responsible for your workload. And remember the key word here is 'communicating', not 'admitting'. If you work to the maximum of your ability, what is there to admit? You should not feel any sense of failure simply because you are facing up to reality. Rather, it is those responsible for turning your workload into work overload who need to admit what they are doing and find ways to rectify it.

If you realize that it is you who is causing the problem then you will need to understand why you are prone to accepting work you should be refusing and find the appropriate way to deal with it. Try using the following chart as a filter to help you, and refine it over time to make it perfectly fit your situation.

What is the work?	Is the work relevant to me?	Am I the best/ most appropriate person for the task?	Do I have the time necessary to begin the task?	Do I have the time to complete the task?	Will the work benefit me?

Remember this

Do not allow your workload to become work overload.

By learning to say 'no' we can stop the problem at source. As the adage maintains, 'Prevention is better than cure', and by ensuring our workload is never allowed to grow and grow to unmanageable proportions we can avoid an unnecessary headache and protect ourselves from unnecessary stress. We can also avoid the time- and energy-consuming necessity of either ploughing through work which we shouldn't really be doing or having to tell the appropriate person that the work won't be getting done.

Reducing volume

One of the greatest barriers to productivity in our modern work lives is the sheer *volume* of things which come our way. The number of communications we receive each and every day can alone threaten to overwhelm us. Add to this all the information which is put before us and it is little wonder that we so often feel like we are swimming in treacle; and that's before we even take account of the volume of tasks and projects with which we are presented – our *actual* work.

In order to make sense of the chaos such volume brings with it, we must first identify what is and what isn't essential. How often have you been in the position of being offered information by a well-meaning boss or colleague and ploughing through it only to discover that it wasn't necessary for you to consume it at all? And how often have you put yourself in the same situation, assimilating and digesting a raft of information because you thought you ought to or that it might perhaps be beneficial, only to realize after a lot of wasted time that it wasn't. By learning to identify what is likely to be useful or essential information, and what is likely to add little direct value and can therefore be ignored, we can rid ourselves of large amounts of unnecessary work and stress while freeing up time and saving energy for more productive pursuits.

And it's not just a case of the volume of work we could and should be avoiding either; it's the toll it takes on us. With every extra demand on our finite resources and each additional bit of clutter we allow into our lives we are slowly becoming choked. By reducing it we will be able to breathe more easily, and become less stressed and more productive. Simply put, simplifying what we do and do not allow into our work lives is a very powerful way of freeing us up to be more productive. Increasing your productivity effectively gives you more time – be sure to use it to best advantage by focusing on the important tasks and completing them on time and to the highest standard.

Next step

In this chapter we have learned that streamlining is a vital tool for anyone trying to boost productivity. In the next chapter, we will look at how to root out those ingrained bad habits that hamper our work lives.

5

Getting into New Habits

In this chapter you will learn:

▸ *The importance of doing one thing at a time and completing it before moving on*

▸ *The importance of leaving work behind – it is detrimental to your productivity to work 24/7*

▸ *The value of positive visualization – by having a clear picture of what you want your day to look and feel like, you can plot a course to help you get there*

▸ *The importance of setting and applying limits – if you try to take on too much, your productivity will suffer on every project*

▸ *How to work on additional projects without sacrificing your productivity – learn to multitask.*

How do you feel?

1 Have you developed habits which are damaging to your productivity?

2 Do you have a clear picture of which habits you need to break – and how to do it?

3 Does multitasking aid or hinder your productivity?

4 Do you know how to protect your productivity from harmful external influences?

5 Do you have a clear picture of what you want to achieve?

'A change in bad habits leads to a change in life.'

Jenny Craig

Stopping damaging work habits

Believe it or not, the process of eating serves as both an excellent analogy for what is going on behind the scenes of your work life and as a practical example of one of the most damaging habits most of us form in order to try to cope with our workload.

When we eat, the biting and swallowing processes take up a fraction of the time, with chewing taking the lion's share. So it is with our work, where opening an email or beginning a project, and sending the email or closing a project, take only a fraction of the time required by the whole task. It is writing the email or actually doing the project – in other words, actioning the task – which takes up most of our time. And just as most of us are guilty of not chewing our food thoroughly, most of us get through our work as quickly as possible because there is so much of it to do, with the inevitable result that it is not always done to the best of our ability.

Finally, the process which actually takes the longest time of all when we eat is the one which is unseen – digestion. And by not taking the appropriate and necessary amount of time to chew, we all too often give ourselves indigestion.

With our work the indigestion is made manifold as **stress**.

By rushing through our work in order to complete it quickly and be able to move on to the next piece (which we will also rush through in order to move on to the next piece, etc., etc.) we are simply storing up trouble for the future. The email we send without giving the subject due consideration and perhaps time for reflection, the project we scrambled through to get it finished on time which meant we couldn't research the subject as thoroughly as we might have done and so on, are unlikely to be accepted without question or revision. So, in fact, what we have done is to create a temporary solution which only leads to problems further down the line.

Remember this: A stitch in time...

Not taking the necessary amount of time required to complete a job properly usually serves only to ensure that it takes longer to complete.

Now imagine taking the time to properly enjoy a meal, chewing the food thoroughly before swallowing, and chewing unhurriedly so as to fully savour each bite, maybe even affording ourselves the luxury of pausing between courses – how much more would we enjoy the meal, how much better would we have prepared the food for our stomachs, and how much less likely would we be to get indigestion from it as a result?

So imagine what our work lives would be like if we were to take this approach – how much more we might enjoy our work, how much better the work we did would be, and how much less likely to cause us stress as a result. What we need to do, then, is to be as choosy about the work we take on as we would be in selecting a meal from a restaurant menu, then ensure that we give ourselves the time and space to complete the work to the best of our ability, ensuring that we are proud of the work we have achieved and that we have avoided unnecessary stress. In this way, we can increase our productivity by completing a job properly before moving on to the next one.

Myth-buster

It is easy to believe that the quicker we can complete a piece of work the more productive we are being. The truth is that 'completing' a piece of work too quickly usually means not having completed it at all, and by having to revisit it and work on it afresh at a later date we are likely to spend more time on it overall. In addition, this disjointed approach to our work slows us further and makes it less likely that the work will be completed to as high a standard as it would have been had we dealt with it fully in the first place.

A PRACTICAL EXAMPLE OF ONE OF THE MOST DAMAGING WORK LIFE HABITS

How many of us can honestly say that we never work while we eat? Or that we never begin planning that next project while going for a walk, playing with our children, or watching television, etc.? In other words, we are not allowing ourselves all-important downtime, the chance to get away from work mentally as well as physically, to get rid of stress and to recharge our batteries.

In order to work to the maximum of our productivity potential we need to allow ourselves the time and space to be unproductive, at least in a work sense. Only that way can we gain the critical distance required to see the bigger picture in our work lives – and, most importantly, to allow ourselves the chance to breathe, to escape from work so that we can resume it refreshed and re-energized.

Quick fix: Recharge your batteries

Analyse your work life and pinpoint those times when you are most likely to succumb to the temptation of working when you should be taking a break from your work. Remember that time away from work is not time spent unproductively – provided you use it to recharge yourself ready to work harder and better later on. Write out a list of these occasions to help you to keep alert to the danger – then act on it!

Case study

'I used to be terrible at leaving work behind – ever. I would always be worrying about what I'd done that day, or thinking about what I should be doing to prepare for tomorrow, etc. It wasn't until I had an appraisal and my manager pointed out to me that my work was suffering as a result of not focusing on just one thing before moving on that I realized that what I was doing was harming my productivity, not helping it. I had fallen into the trap of thinking that the more I did the better. I now realize that it's the more I do really well the better.'

Remember this: Having downtime is not being unproductive

Not working all the time does not mean you are not being productive; it means you are allowing yourself vital space to be as productive as possible.

Just as we need to allow ourselves the space to leave work behind, we need to allow ourselves the space to concentrate on one thing at a time if we are to do it to the best of our ability – in other words, if we are to do it in the most productive way possible. So even if we eat in such a way as to give ourselves physically the best possible chance of processing the food properly and avoiding indigestion, if we do not allow ourselves to concentrate on this one activity alone we are likely to still end up with indigestion.

So it is with our work – if we do not allow ourselves the space and time to concentrate on one project or piece of work exclusively, but rather flit from one thing to the next and back again in a nervous and hurried cycle (which it is all too easy to believe is allowing us to be productive just by keeping us busy), then we can hardly be surprised if we find ourselves constantly suffering from stress – or 'work indigestion'!

Positive visualization

> 'Positive thinking is the key to success in business, education, pro football, anything that you can mention. I go out there thinking that I'm going to complete every pass.'
>
> Ron Jaworski

This is a technique much favoured by athletes and sportsmen and women who use it to help them to perform on the field of play to the best of their ability by thinking through the most positive outcome and visualizing the steps required to get them there. By using the same technique, you can ensure that you start every piece of work and every day in the right frame of mind and with the best possible chance of a successful outcome.

1   **Eliminating negative thoughts.** All negative thoughts are barriers to your ability to achieve a successful outcome since they create doubt and fear about your ability to succeed or the worth of the project as a whole. These will be damaging to your productivity and so must be identified, blocked and eradicated.

2   **Visualizing the route.** You will need to think through what it is you hope to achieve and break it down into manageable steps – and you will need to ensure that you think through the entire route. For a footballer this might begin with arriving at the stadium, then getting changed and warming up, then playing the match, while being sure to visualize all the component parts including:

▷ teamwork

▷ running at speed without tiring

▷ scoring

▷ what to do if things start to go wrong

▷ hearing the final whistle securing the victory.

What it entails for you depends, of course, upon your work situation, which will be unique and is unlikely to be as similar to that of a footballer! At the highest levels of the professional game footballers are taught to do this before each and every match and it is just as important for you to do this every day in *your* work life – the more you practise, the better at it you will become.

3 **Picturing a perfect result.** Finally, you should picture the most successful outcome. Just as footballers are taught to picture what ultimate victory will look and feel like, so you should get into the habit of imagining and feeling what it will be like when your work is finished with a perfect result.

By following these simple steps you can easily put yourself in the right frame of mind to help you to accomplish your goals quickly and efficiently. With practice you will be able to harness the power of your mind to give you the best possible chance of succeeding in everything you do – and this can be a very powerful tool indeed.

Try It now: Plot your course to success

Try thinking through your current project, or the next piece of work you have to do. Imagine it from every angle and from the beginning (or where you are with it at the moment) to its conclusion. See it being a great success and try to imagine how that makes you feel. Then determine what you will need to do to ensure it happens and plot your course to success. Use the following questions to help you.

✳ What negative thoughts do I have about my job?
✳ What negative thoughts do I have about my current project?
✳ How can I eliminate these negative thoughts?
✳ What is the best route to success in my work?
✳ How can I break this down into manageable steps?
✳ What would constitute a perfect result?
✳ What steps do I need to take to make this a reality?

Setting limits – and how to apply them

Nobody, no matter how motivated they are and how much energy they have, has an infinite capacity for work; and by taking on more work than is good for us we are simply pushing ourselves past the tipping point of maximum productivity and limiting our ability to get things done effectively. It is therefore extremely important to set workable limits, to adhere to them rigidly, and to review them frequently. You will need to be aware that the process of workplace limitation works on both a macro and micro level and will need to be employed not only for each project you are engaged in (and the total number of projects you take on) but for each and every aspect of your work life which can threaten to overwhelm you if it is not appropriately controlled.

Remember this

Simplicity is a workplace necessity.

> 'Achieve success in any area of life by identifying the optimum strategies and repeating them until they become habits.'
>
> Charles J. Givens

Macro versus micro limitations

The easiest way to see the difference between these is to see them in action. Let us take as an example a project which is concerned with providing innovation in a marketing context to a client who makes crisps and snacks. The role of the person we are looking at is the account manager of a marketing agency responsible for this client (we'll call him 'David').

MACRO LIMITATIONS

The first and very significant challenge David faces is that, because innovation is concerned with creativity and ideas generation, there is no fixed endpoint; in other words, there is no limit to the number of creative ideas, opportunities, new products, etc. which could be dreamed up by the innovation team. David will therefore have to set some arbitrary limitations to prevent the project spiralling out of control. Not only does this set a limitation to the length of time the project will take (which is crucial as the client will be expecting a finished product at some point!) but it also helps to focus the team, and to ensure that the innovation streams they pursue are equally focused.

As these are large, general limitations they fall under the category of macro limitations. David might, for example, decide that the team will have one week to come up with as many ideas as possible – after that, the process will shift to one of sorting, filtering and categorization to see just how many good ideas there are and to ditch the rest. He might then allocate three days to revisit this process (now they have seen which ideas are working best), thereby ensuring that they have every opportunity to come up with the very best innovation.

In this way, David has allowed a total of eight days to accomplish a task which might otherwise have been allowed to drift into weeks if not months. As the project then moves forward into a different phase, one in which the team will need to work up the ideas to make them ready for presentation to the client, David will need to allocate a set time period in which this must be accomplished, and so on for the rest of the project. In many ways, setting macro limitations is the easy part since it is really just disciplined project planning, and while there must be some flexibility in the plan this can be easily managed by utilizing a degree of fluidity in the planning.

MICRO LIMITATIONS

More difficult is setting micro limitations. Let us suppose that David is in a situation where he cannot afford himself the luxury of not checking his emails during the day and that he must also keep his mobile on in case the clients want a progress report. Let us suppose, too, that David is at the mercy of his bosses and other colleagues who frequently solicit his opinion on a variety of topics, including other live projects, because they know how good he is and naturally want to get his input.

Each of these interruptions to David's workflow will have a negative impact on his productivity. Unfortunately, it's not as simple as this, though, because they will also have a negative impact on the productivity of the rest of his team, and therefore the entire project. However, to ignore the clients would also be detrimental to the project, and to refuse the request for help from his bosses and colleagues would be detrimental to their projects.

This requirement to balance the needs of several things at once is a real concern for most people given the structures within which most people work today. David must therefore plan a way to navigate through this potential minefield, providing valuable input wherever possible but without stretching himself to the point where his productivity will be diminished. So how can he achieve this? The answer lies in setting and sticking to a series of micro limitations.

What are micro limitations?

Simply put, micro limitations are the limits put in place on any number of things whose frequent and unregulated interruptions would threaten productivity. These include:

▶ sending or responding to **emails**

▶ making or receiving **phone calls**

▶ assisting **colleagues**

▶ providing **project updates** for bosses, clients and colleagues

▶ providing **fresh input** to other projects for bosses

▶ updating **company blogs**

▶ leaving the current piece of work **to begin or continue with another piece of work** (e.g. putting together a proposal or a pitch for a new piece of work)

▶ checking or responding to any **social media** (e.g. Facebook, Twitter, YouTube, etc.).

We'll look at each of these in turn below to see how they can best be managed to prevent them damaging your productivity.

Remember this: Regulate interruptions

By executing self-imposed limitations to what you allow into your work life it is possible to regulate the number and flow of disruptions and distractions. This will enable you to gain control of your day-to-day work structure and ensure that you can focus on your work unimpeded and uninterrupted.

SENDING OR RESPONDING TO EMAILS

Let us look first at the issue of emails, since this is one of the most common workplace bugbears for many people. Simply dealing with the flow of emails as and when they occur is a recipe for disaster. While it might seem like this is a sensible approach – indeed, a *productive* approach – since it means that the emails will be dealt with in a timely fashion and never allowed to build up, it in fact necessitates a constant stream of interruptions to your work.

Since we have already seen that David, like many of us, is not in a position simply to not check his emails throughout the day and leave them until the end of the day (the easiest and almost always best solution where possible), he must instead decide on a sensible way of managing how he will deal with his emails. He might, for instance, decide that he will only check his emails once per hour. In this way, he is not constantly distracted and sidetracked by having to leave his work and refocus on whatever it is that his emails are about, and he is not continually on tenterhooks wondering if another email will suddenly ping into his inbox forcing him to leave his work to deal with it.

By deciding that he will only check his emails once every hour David is freeing himself up to concentrate on his work the rest of the time. This is a great way to implement an important micro limitation to your work, thereby safeguarding your productivity.

Myth-buster

Not checking your emails continually as and when they come in does not mean that you are being unproductive and storing up trouble for the future. What it does mean is that you are taking control of your workflow – thereby maximizing your productivity.

Furthermore, David might decide that it is a sensible approach to answer only the most urgent emails each time he does check leaving any remaining until the end of the day. In this way, he is safeguarding his time and his productivity by implementing a further, or secondary, micro limitation. By doing so, David not only ensures that he does not spend too much time on his hourly email catch-up but, by forcing himself to choose the most crucial emails, he is implementing a method of focusing on what is really important.

A further benefit to this approach is that the people who email David on a regular basis will begin to understand that their emails will only be responded to during the day if they are of sufficient importance. Over time, David will see a decrease in the number of non-crucial emails he is receiving. A further micro limitation which David might choose to implement is to let it be known generally among his company that he does not wish to be copied into every email conversation which may or may not have some tangential bearing on his work.

This is a trap into which many people fall. By not wanting to miss out on what is going on, or by feeling that not being added to a recipient list for an email conversation may be taken the wrong way by colleagues or may leave them at a disadvantage, people all too often become subject to a myriad email streams which have little or no direct relevance to them but all of which take time, effort and energy to wade through. In this way, they are not empowering you by ensuring that you have your finger on the pulse of what is going on everywhere and all the time, but instead they become hugely detrimental to your productivity by getting in the way of what is really important. Thus setting sensible micro limitations will not only safeguard your productivity but, by helping you to focus on what is important, they will also aid your ability to prioritize.

Remember this: Deal with non-urgent emails at the end of the day

Limiting the number of emails to which you respond throughout the day does not mean the others go unread but that they do not need to be dealt with right away. They will still be there at the end of the day when they can be answered without disrupting your work.

MAKING OR RECEIVING PHONE CALLS

Any unregulated interruptions to your working day will impair your productivity, and another source of potential continual interruptions to which most people are subject is telephone calls. Again, let us suppose that David is not in a position simply to not notice (or pretend that he hasn't noticed!) whether or not his phone is ringing throughout the day and leave responding to voicemails to the end of the day (the easiest and almost always best solution where possible). Given that he has no option but to deal with his calls, he must instead decide on a sensible way of managing how he will deal with them.

The term 'fielding telephone calls' is often applied and it is a good one because it implies that the calls need to be dealt with but that this doesn't necessarily mean by answering them. In much the same way as David needs to manage his emails (but with one additional layer of immediacy), he must decide which calls must be dealt with straightaway and which can be left. He needs to prioritize them in the following order:

▶ calls which must be taken

▶ calls which can be left to go to voicemail – upon checking voicemail, he then needs to decide:

  ▷ which calls needs to be returned

  ▷ which calls warrant a response other than a return phone call (it is often quicker and easier to send an email)

  ▷ which calls can be left without a reply of any sort.

David will need to be extremely disciplined about which calls he puts into which category – not an easy task given that he will need to do this as and when they occur and will only have a few seconds – the length of time it takes for the phone to ring before it goes to voicemail – in which to make his decision. Because any calls which must be taken will cause an immediate disruption to David's work, they must be kept to an absolute minimum. It can be very tempting to answer calls which should really be left – perhaps because you think they will only take a couple of minutes and will save you the job of having to call back later, or because they are from someone you like and would really like to talk to. However, because each unavoidably breaks your concentration and focus from the work you were undertaking when the phone rang, they absolutely *must* be left to go to voicemail if that is at all possible. Those which fall into the second category – i.e. those which don't need to be taken straight away but which do warrant being returned at some point – must be dealt with in the same way as email traffic.

David therefore has the opportunity to answer all his calls at a time of his choosing and it is usually best not to do this every hour as with emails but instead to limit it to just once or twice per day. This is because it is quicker and easier to fire off emails than to make telephone calls, and also because with emails you are in sole charge of their content whereas with telephone calls it is very difficult to prevent the person on the other end of the line from covering multiple topics, not just those which were in their voicemail. In this way it is all too easy to find yourself spending more time on these calls then you had envisaged and also to find that they are covering topics for which you had not prepared yourself.

ASSISTING COLLEAGUES

This can be one of the most difficult areas in which to set limits, for two reasons:

1 You will naturally want to help your colleagues as best you can even if doing so is detrimental to your productivity.

2 Your colleagues are right there, a physical presence in your space, and therefore hard to ignore!

The simplest way to get around this is to implement rules to safeguard your productivity and ensure that these become widely known. In this example, David needs to get the word out among his colleagues that he would prefer not to be disturbed during the day but is happy to see anyone at the end of the day, ensuring that they are all aware of his need and desire to focus on the task at hand. Providing he manages this properly, David should find that his colleagues do not disturb him unless it is a real emergency, and therefore entirely appropriate.

A knock-on effect of this approach, and a distinct added bonus, is that David's colleagues will understand the pressures he is under and his need to focus and concentrate his productivity on the task at hand, and with any luck they will not only respect his desire to avoid a stream of constant interruptions, but they might actually be in a position to offer him some practical help.

Quick fix: At the end of the day...

Try telling your colleagues that you would really appreciate it if, when possible, they did not ask for your opinion or assistance until the end of the day. Even people who think that this would be impossible in their situation, or that doing so might cause offence, are very often pleasantly surprised.

PROVIDING PROJECT UPDATES FOR BOSSES, CLIENTS AND COLLEAGUES

In much the same way as David must manage his colleagues' needs and expectations, he must manage those of his bosses. It is, of course, entirely appropriate and to be expected that David's bosses will want updates and progress reports on the state of the current project. Equally, this is to be expected of clients and of other people working on the same project. Again, the key for David is to ensure that he manages this appropriately so that everybody is kept in the loop and feels fully informed and fully involved in the project without this impacting negatively on his ability to push the project forward – in other words on his productivity.

The easiest way to accomplish this is to arrange with all those concerned that you will provide them with regular updates. In this way, by you going to them and not them coming to you, you can provide the updates at a time of your choosing and avoid unnecessary interruptions. Try to ensure that the updates are regular but brief, thus avoiding you having to spend a lot of time on them while ensuring that everybody it concerns knows when the updates will arrive. Provided that the updates do arrive punctually, people will have no need to press you for information at other times. Try to ensure that you schedule these updates at a time when you:

▶ are unlikely to be under project time pressures

▶ at the beginning of the day when you are fresh and when the recipients will have time to digest your reports.

This also helps to ensure that you do not get pestered during the day for a report which people have come to expect on that day – for example, if people know that you will provide a report every Wednesday, there is a danger that they will hassle you for this report on Wednesday during the day if it is your habit not to provide it until the evening. By ensuring that they have it first thing this can easily be prevented.

PROVIDING FRESH INPUT TO OTHER PROJECTS FOR BOSSES

This can be one of the most difficult areas to deal with, owing in no small measure to the fact that it is one over which you have limited control. One of the most important things is to ensure that your bosses are fully and continually apprised of the state of the project on which you are working:

▶ Try to ensure that they know **the extent of your workload.**

▶ Try to ensure that they are fully aware of **the value of the work** you are undertaking.

▶ Where possible, try to make sure that they are aware of **the extent of the support** you are receiving.

By ensuring that your bosses know exactly what you're dealing with in your current project they will, with any luck, try not to pick your brains on other matters too frequently. Of course, because you are a valued member of the team, it is likely that they will want your input on other projects from time to time, so try to make sure that you have a small cushion of time built into your project to allow for this.

UPDATING COMPANY BLOGS

If you are a contributor to a company blog (or, indeed, if you are the blog's sole author), you will need to set aside time to write your articles. Let us suppose that David is the sole author of a company blog. In order to continue to operate in his other company roles with maximum productivity, while ensuring that the company blog is as good as it can be, David will need to implement a structure to make this happen – and then stick to it. He will need to decide:

▶ **how many words** each contribution to the blog should be.

▶ **what subject** the blog will be on (ensuring that he has plenty to say about this without sacrificing his productivity by wasting time racking his brains to come up with opinions on subjects with which he is unfamiliar or uninterested).

▶ **how frequently** he will update the blog.

▶ **when** he will update the blog.

▶ on **a definite endpoint** to the blog.

By deciding on and implementing the above as a set workplace structure, David can ensure that the blog is completed in a timely fashion and to a high standard without impacting on his other work – in other words, without impacting on his productivity. Indeed, if David has chosen a subject which interests him, and preferably one which can use the current project to provide insight or stimulus material, then he may well find that, far from impacting negatively on his productivity, it does just the opposite, inspiring and stimulating him in his work while also providing an interesting diversion and convenient break without breaking his focus.

They say that a change is as good as a rest and this is a great way of implementing this philosophy in your day to day work life.

LEAVING THE CURRENT PIECE OF WORK TO BEGIN, OR CONTINUE WITH, ANOTHER PIECE OF WORK

It is an inescapable fact of modern work practices that sometimes leaving the current piece of work altogether to begin work on something completely different is simply unavoidable. The two most common causes of this are:

1 the requirement **to put together a proposal or pitch** for a new piece of work

2 the need **to revisit a previous piece of work** to make adjustments or implement updates for a client.

When this happens, it needs to be carefully managed. Let us suppose that David, knee deep in an existing project, has no choice but to put together a proposal for a future prospective client. The first thing David must do is to decide when is the best time to leave the current piece of work and to turn his mind to something completely different. With any luck there will be a natural break opportunity in his work stream, so the first thing he must do is to try to identify this and schedule the new work around it. This may mean that he has to delay the new piece of work for a short period until such an opportunity presents itself, so it is important to liaise with the future potential client to ensure that they know when the proposal is likely to arrive.

The next step David must take in order to try to minimize the disruptive impact of the proposal is to complete it in one go. It could be extremely damaging to David's overall productivity if he allows the work on the new proposal to be a constant, albeit intermittent, interruption over a sustained period of time. Lastly, David must be very clear about exactly what the proposal should contain and crucially how long, or how detailed, it needs to be. In this way, David will avoid the productivity-diminishing trap of putting in more work and spending more time on the new proposal than is necessary. Just as importantly, David needs to ensure that he starts work on the new proposal with a definite endpoint in mind, so that when he reaches it he can mentally put it in his 'done' box – then forget it and move on.

So the process should be:

1 Identify the **best time** to break from the current project in order to work on the new proposal.

2 Ensure that the time you have identified as the most suitable for completing the new project is sufficient to ensure that it can be completed in **one fell swoop.**

3 Be clear from the outset exactly what the proposal should contain and how long it should be. Determine the **endpoint** for the proposal before you begin.

Quick fix: Identify a break in your schedule

If you have to complete a proposal or pitch, try to identify a suitable break in your schedule as soon as possible – even if the break is a long way off. By communicating this to your boss and to the client, you can ring-fence the time in between, confident in the knowledge that all parties have bought into this approach. In this way, you will effectively ring-fence your productivity.

CHECKING OR RESPONDING TO ANY SOCIAL MEDIA

Assuming that this is a necessary part of David's work life (e.g. that the company for which he works maintains an online social media presence and that he has been allocated the task of keeping at least one of these communication tools updated and relevant), he needs to implement a rigid and defined structure which will allow him to do this without negatively impacting on his productivity in the other areas of his work life. In order to do this, David needs to consider the following:

▶ How **frequently** must the task be undertaken?

▶ How **long** will it take to complete the task each time?

▶ When is the **best time** to complete the task?

For this example, let us suppose that David's job is to keep the company's Facebook profile up to date, and to keep the content relevant and interesting to its followers. David might therefore answer the above set of questions as follows:

▶ How frequently must the task be undertaken?

   ▷ *Primary* – each time there is a new and relevant development to post, either from within the company or in the world of marketing and advertising in general. Twice per week will be sufficient.

   ▷ *Secondary* – each time a client, customer, colleague or interested follower leaves a post which requires a reply. This needs to be done on an ad hoc basis.

▶ How long will it take to complete the task each time?

   ▷ *Primary* – these posts needs to be carefully thought through and will often require the addition of images or web links. Each post should therefore be given 30 minutes.

   ▷ *Secondary* – these will typically be answering a question or query, or responding in the company's house style to a comment made by a visitor. These are sporadic and rarely are two such posts left on the same day. These should take no more than 10 minutes.

▶ When is the best time to complete the task?

   ▷ *Primary* – these should be completed on the same day and at approximately the same time each week – so, first thing every Tuesday and Friday.

   ▷ *Secondary* – questions or comments should be acknowledged and responded to as soon as possible in order to ensure that the company appears interested and to make sure that its viewpoint is presented as quickly as possible – so, last thing every day.

By implementing this structure David is safeguarding his productivity. Remember that these tasks are not part of his main job, the area where he wishes to focus his efforts, but an addition. If David did not establish such a firm routine for dealing with this aspect of his work, he would almost certainly find himself checking the company's Facebook page either at frequent intervals throughout the day or periodically as and when it occurred to him or he found time to do it.

Either of these has the potential to be equally damaging to David's productivity. With the first of these, the total length of time David spends checking the company's Facebook page is certain to exceed the length of time it would take if he checked it just once per day and twice on Tuesdays and Fridays. Not only this, but his concentration and focus would be broken at frequent intervals throughout the day. With the second of these, the problem of broken focus and concentration still applies, with the added complication that the Facebook page is likely to be neglected for days at a time.

David also needs to consider not only his overall productivity (which will impact the main strand of his work most of all) but also his productivity in managing the company's Facebook page. By defining and implementing rigid structures to manage this, therefore, David ensures that his productivity is maximized in both areas.

Try it now: Plot your course to success

Try creating your own micro limitations by asking yourself the following questions:

* What macro limitations do I need to impose in my work life?
* What micro limitations do I need to impose in my work life?
* What steps do I need to take to make these happen?
* What are the potential hurdles I may have to overcome?
* How can I best prepare for these?

'Simple productivity' versus 'targeted productivity'

One final and overarching matter which needs to be considered in order to reach an overall level of excellent productivity is that there is a substantial difference between simple productivity and productivity which is focused and targeted – the latter being so much more effective and therefore likely to achieve a greater degree of true productivity. So what is the difference between 'productivity' and 'targeted productivity'?

SIMPLE PRODUCTIVITY

While responding to any number of calls on your time and expertise as the day progresses may in itself be productive – that is, in each case you may be adding a valuable contribution to a piece of work – it will have no productive effect on the original aim. In this way, while such instances cannot be classed as *unproductive*, their productivity is *limited*. Look at it this way – if you were to take the combined productivity of all these little pieces throughout a day and add them together, you would quickly see that their combined total is nowhere near that of a day spent focusing on one task.

TARGETED PRODUCTIVITY

By focusing on one particular task and concentrating all your efforts on that and ensuring that interruptions are kept to a minimum you will truly maximize your productivity. It is therefore imperative that you are not content with simply being productive but that you are productive in a targeted manner so that the piece of work which is your focus is the sole recipient of your productivity. In this way, you can truly maximize your productivity.

Next step

In this chapter we have learned how to break those bad habits that keep us from maximizing our productivity – for example, responding to email and phone calls without first assessing their importance. Next we will turn to the key role that careful planning plays in producing a successful strategy for productivity.

6

Targets, Motivation and Planning

In this chapter you will learn to:

▷ *Clearly define your targets to give yourself every opportunity to succeed and avoid becoming unnecessarily sidetracked*

▷ *Identify potential problems and devise coping strategies to minimize any disruptions to completing each project on time and to budget*

▷ *Continually reassess to keep track of your progress and be sure to notice any hindrances to your productivity as soon as they arise – and deal with them*

▷ *Be realistic in your expectations and plan properly*

▷ *Motivate yourself by providing yourself with tangible rewards for achieving your targets.*

How do you feel?

1 Do you know exactly what you want to achieve, and by when?

2 Are your targets realistic, manageable and achievable?

3 What are the main barriers to your being productive?

4 How will you measure your productivity progress?

5 How will you motivate and reward yourself?

Clearly defining your targets

In order to maximize your productivity, it is essential you have a set of clearly defined targets and a clear plan of how and when you will achieve them, and that you revise them frequently to ensure that you're on track. In order for your targets and plans to provide a useful yardstick of your productivity you will need to ensure that they are realistic, clearly defined and measurable.

Remember this: Hoping is not enough!

Simply *hoping* you will achieve your goals is guaranteed to impair your productivity. You need to *plan*.

One of the main reasons for a lack of productivity is the lack of a clear vision. If you're vague as to what it is you plan to achieve, when you plan to achieve it, and how you will do so, you are unlikely to succeed quickly and efficiently, if at all. It is therefore crucial that you define your targets at the *outset* of any project.

You will need to:

▶ determine your **objectives**

▶ define the **parameters**

▶ set a **realistic timescale**

▶ identify potential **barriers** and **roadblocks**

   ▷ learn how to identify them early

   ▷ outline coping strategies for dealing with them

▶ put in place **measurement criteria**

- periodically **assess your progress**
- determine how to **cope with any setbacks.**

Let's look at an example. Anna spends a portion of her time working from home and has one room which serves as her office. However, it also serves as a general household dumping ground and she has identified that tidying it and redecorating it in a more workplace style and keeping it free from anything not work-related will help her to increase her productivity. Her plan might look something like this:

Objectives *To tidy and redecorate the office, and to purge it of anything not work-related.*

Parameters *To make the office neater, work-focused, and feeling more like a workspace. Allocate a budget of £500.00.*

Timescale *Begin this week, complete within six months.*

Potential barriers and roadblocks *The urge to sort out all the clutter which isn't work-related rather than just removing it; the need to find somewhere else to work during the redecoration; the need for somewhere to store all the work-related items while the office is being painted and somewhere to permanently store all the non-work-related clutter. Is budget sufficient?*

Coping strategies *Be satisfied with sorting work-related clutter only and just tidying everything else - put in place a separate plan for sorting the non-work-related clutter; use living room as temporary office; put clutter in bedroom during redecoration and store unsorted (non-work-related) clutter in garage.*

Measurement criteria *Is everything on schedule? Is it looking and feeling the way I want it to? Am I keeping to the budget?*

Assess your progress *Weekly.*

Coping with setbacks *As they occur.*

Quick fix: Five-minute plan

Your initial plan needn't be pages and pages long (the thought of which might provide an excuse to procrastinate!), so just grab a pen and a piece of paper and limit yourself to five minutes. This will force you to focus on only the most important areas and provide you with a useful framework from which to work when compiling a more detailed plan later on.

'In preparing for battle I have always found that plans are useless, but planning is indispensable.'

Dwight D. Eisenhower

Why identifying potential problems and devising coping strategies is so important

Identifying potential problems and deciding how best to deal with them is absolutely critical to increasing your productivity. In this example Anna has realized that as she clears the office ready for the redecoration she will be tempted to sort through everything, whether work-related or not, rather than simply move it out of the way. This is perhaps a worthwhile task in its own right but it isn't part of the project she's undertaking and so it must be listed as a separate project. The danger is that things like this can quickly and easily spiral out of control...

> While clearing the office Anna notices a coffee machine which she has never used. She decides to sell it but then wonders if her sister would like to have it. She phones her sister who doesn't have time to talk as one of her children is unwell and needs collecting from school. Anna puts the coffee machine back where it was making a mental note to call her sister again later and notices it was resting on an exercise bench which should be stored in the garden shed. However, before she can take it there she knows she'll have to clear out the shed (and while she's doing that she might

as well make room in the garage where the clutter from her office and from the shed will be stored).

While clearing the shed Anna notices an old bicycle which she doesn't need and decides to place an advert in the local paper. She switches on her computer to look up the paper's contact details and decides to place an ad online, too, but sees that she has an email which needs answering about the following week's conference call. Before she can do that, however, she'll need to contact the other three people involved, one of whom will also want to know where she's at on another project for which she'll need to contact a supplier and wait for their response...

And so on. Days can pass in this way and Anna will still be no nearer to achieving her goal of redecorating the office than she was when she started. This could easily have been avoided if Anna had only stuck to the task at hand and not allowed herself to become sidetracked by other tasks. Moreover, she will have fallen into one of the most common counter-productivity traps – transference.

Transference

Anna's goal was to clear the office ready for the redecoration, a task which could and should have been completed in a couple of hours. Instead, she has spent the entire afternoon on it and is no closer to completing it now than she was at the outset. She has also identified other tasks, both work-related and non-work-related, and has begun these but not finished any of them. The impact of this can most clearly be seen in a spider diagram: see Figure 6.1.

Seen in this way several things become apparent:

▶ Anna has moved from one clearly defined task to a dizzying, unfocused to-do list.

▶ She hasn't actually achieved anything (no tasks have been completed).

▶ She is mixing work life with home life – a damaging lack of focus.

- Her *approach* lacks structure and therefore –

  ▷ her day lacks structure

  ▷ her activities lack structure

- She has unearthed numerous additional tasks making her feel 'snowed under'.

- Her way of dealing with things is creating, not solving, problems.

Solution – these problems could easily have been avoided if Anna had simply identified them, or their potential, early on and devised an appropriate coping strategy. By devising and implementing a coping strategy of just moving the non-work-related items for now but allocating sorting them to a separate, future project (and allocating a specific time to do this), Anna can focus on achieving her goals on the current project – and then focus on achieving her goals on the next project at the appropriate time. This maximizes her productivity and ensures that both projects have much more chance of success.

Remember this: Make your parameters clear

By being clear as to the parameters of any given project – no matter how big or small it may be – and strict about sticking to them, you will give yourself every chance of succeeding in the most productive manner.

Next Anna will need to put her plan into a framework which allows her to monitor her progress. This should be kept simple so that it's clear and quick and easy to use. If it doesn't tell you straight away whether or not you're on track to meet your goal, you're less likely to refer to it often – something you'll need to do in order to catch any problems early on. The best way to do this is to draw up a 'productivity chart'.

Quick fix: Create a template productivity chart

If you create a basic template for your productivity chart, you will be able to make multiple copies, one for each new project.

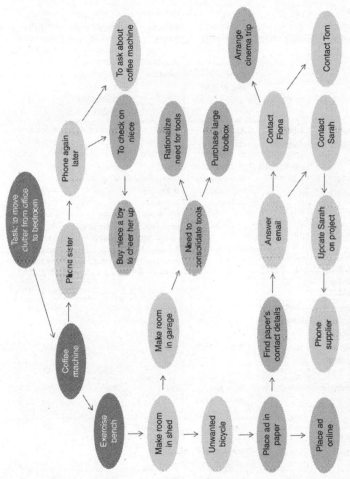

Figure 6.1 Spider diagram – transference

	Week	Month	Quarter	Year	Ongoing
Completion date	May 7	June 1	July 31	April 30	
What do I want to achieve?	Tidy office	Paint office	Re-carpet and refurnish office	Have new office bedded-in	Keep office tidy
What are the likely barriers?	Lots of stuff which needs really sorting, not just moving	During redecoration: – Nowhere to store office items – need somewhere else to work	Late delivery; storage; finding time to choose new furniture	Urge to keep re-arranging; keeping on buying additional furnishings; breakages; insufficient budget	Lack of time; too much 'stuff'; hoarding
Coping strategies	Agree separate project for dealing with this	Agree with partner use of bedroom & living room as temporary store and workspace	Agree delivery and fitting in good time; accept deliveries only when office is ready for them; choose furniture at weekends	Be strict – get the arrangement right first time; only add to furnishings if really necessary; repair or replace as needed	Agree time to tidy – 10 minutes per day; keep accessories to a minimum; do not keep unnecessary items!
Am I on track…?					
Week ending 04/05	Yes – target achieved	Yes	Yes	Yes	N/A
Week ending 11/05	N/A	Yes	Yes	Yes	N/A
Week ending 18/05	N/A	No – not enough paint	Yes	Yes	N/A
Week ending 25/05	N/A	No – room requires extra coat of paint	No – carpet delivery delayed	No – 3 week delay	N/A
Week ending 01/06	N/A	No – target missed by 4 days	Yes – delivery back on track	Yes	N/A

Sample productivity chart – Project: redecorate the office

Drawing up a chart like this enables you to see quickly and clearly if you are on target, ahead or behind schedule. It also allows you to track your progress. This will not only help you to monitor where you have got to (versus where you had planned to get to) at each stage but will also provide a useful history of your productivity. This can then be used to help you to diagnose where you were doing well or poorly, and how you can improve your strategy for other projects.

Use the following guidelines:

▶ When completing the 'Am I on track...?' sections it is important to:

▷ be **honest** about your progress

▷ use this as an opportunity to **re-evaluate** the situation

▶ If you're falling behind:

▷ ensure you are clear about the **reasons** for this

▷ set in place a **strategy** to correct it.

▶ Each time you complete one of the stages, on time, **reward yourself** to celebrate your success. By deciding early on what this reward will be, you can provide useful motivation to help you keep going when the going gets tough.

▶ If you're falling behind, identify the reasons why and determine how you will remedy them. Then action it.

Continual reassessment

It's very difficult to accurately predict what you might achieve by the end of the year if you don't have a clear idea of what you can achieve in a quarter, a month, a week and even a day. By understanding and defining what you can realistically expect to achieve, given a high but obtainable level of productivity, you can begin to gauge where you should be at any given point. By comparing this to where you actually are you will be able to measure your productivity quickly and accurately.

The key is to ensure that the targets you set yourself are realistic in order to ensure that you are continually heading in the right direction, and at the required speed. It is far too easy (and commonplace) to get to a point on the calendar and wonder, in a regretful tone, where the year has gone and why you did not reach any of the targets you set – in other words, why you were so unproductive. It is vitally important to be crystal clear as to what you want to achieve, and by when, and although this might change as things evolve and circumstances dictate fluctuations in your anticipated course and speed, having a very clear vision and knowing the course you want to steer will enable you to keep track of your progress and keep things on target.

If you are determined to maximize your productivity, you must be willing to continually assess your progress on any given task to ensure that you are achieving as much as you ought to be. How often you check your progress and reassess your level of productivity will depend on a number of factors (the size of the tasks involved, how long it will take you to check, your preferred workday structure, etc.), but at the very least it should be done at the end of every week – and many people find it useful, and motivating, to check on a daily basis.

Case study

'When I first adopted the policy of measuring my productivity I did so at the end of each week but quickly found that I was falling short of what I'd hoped I would achieve. With analysis (and a lot of honesty!) I realized that this was because I was being a lot more productive on Fridays when I knew I would be checking my progress at the end of the day, but the rest of the week I wasn't achieving what I needed to. Now I check twice every day, at lunchtime and at the end of the day. It only takes a couple of minutes and the increase in my productivity has been amazing.'

Setting realistic targets

'The pessimist complains about the wind; the optimist expects it to change; the realist adjusts the sails.'

William Arthur Ward

One of the key strategies to employ in order to maximize your productivity is to ensure the targets you set for yourself really are realistic given your available time, resources, experience, ability, the prevailing conditions etc. Above all, be honest with yourself and be tough where you need to be. It will save a lot of unnecessary and completely avoidable disappointment later on.

If your expectations are unrealistically high then you are simply setting yourself up to fail. Worse still, you are creating a framework which could very well prevent you succeeding. There is nothing quite so demotivating as periodically looking at what you've achieved versus what you had planned to achieve and knowing that you cannot possibly attain your goals. This is a sure-fire way to impair your productivity.

Remember this: Be realistic about your targets

Aiming unrealistically high is a great way to make you feel like a failure even if you are doing well. So be tough with yourself and realistic, even if that means setting your sights a little lower than you would like to.

One school of thought suggests that the easiest way to ensure you always reach your targets, and to avoid disappointment, is simply to aim low! However, if your targets are too low then your productivity will be impaired by having achieved them quickly and easily, leaving yourself nothing to shoot for and knowing in your heart of hearts that the only reason for your apparent success is that you cheated yourself in the first place – just as demotivating as setting your targets too high.

So you need to ensure your targets are as realistic as possible. What those are will, of course, depend on a huge number of factors unique to you and your situation, but it is worth spending the necessary time to ensure you get them as accurate as possible and be prepared to revise them periodically.

Wall planners are a great way to increase your productivity. They allow you to plot what you plan to achieve throughout the year and keep your targets and deadlines in sight at all times. This is a great way to ensure that not a day goes by when you are not reminded of where you are, where you want to be, and by when. If you start falling behind, it is an inescapable reminder, which is no bad thing, and if you are ahead of schedule it can be wonderfully motivating. It is also useful to have your entire year's targets and plans laid out before you so you can see the big picture at a glance, and it helps to prevent any looming targets or deadlines coming as a surprise.

Remember this: There are no exceptions!

Don't fall into the trap of thinking that you're the one person who can get away with not planning. You're not – no one is.

Quick fix: Buy a wall planner

Buy yourself a wall planner right away – just having it on your wall will inspire you to fill it in and provide a useful spur to increasing your productivity. Remember – Proper Planning and Preparation Prevents Poor Performance!

Exercise: Write your own obituary

This is a self-actualizing exercise.

STAGE 1: WRITE DOWN YOUR DESTINATION

First, you need to write a brief paragraph describing how your life might be summed up at any given stage – for example:

▶ What will you be doing?

▶ What will your day-to-day work comprise?

- What will your salary be?
- Where will you be living?
  - What sort of property will you have?
- What will you have achieved...
  - in your work life?
  - in your private life?

Write it in as much detail as you feel is necessary to fully convey what you hope to accomplish. It is your life, it is your vision, it is your dream. So go ahead and write the future. Prescribe all the elements of your successes. Ambition is no bad thing here, so by all means aim high – just remember you need to be realistic, too. This document, if well thought out and pragmatic, should form a point of reference for you for the future, a control chart against which you can map your progress – but realism is crucial. If your targets were beyond the bounds of what might reasonably be achieved with a lot of hard work, dedication and productivity, then its worth is dramatically diminished and you are simply setting yourself up for a fall.

As you can see from the following examples, 'obituaries' can come in all shapes and sizes and they need not be long and complicated – just make sure that yours is the right length and complexity for you.

> **Paul Adams** is a dedicated family man and an expert painter and decorator. He is also an outstanding sportsman; a regular fixture in the Brighton marathon, a club-level hockey player, and captain of the 2012 Aurora Cup-winning cricket team. He enjoys extensive travel and upon retiring realized his long-held dream of completing a world cruise.

> **Laura McWinley – 40th birthday.** Laura arrived home after two rewarding years in Sydney just in time for the birthday celebrations she always hoped to have, a giant party. She has completed her MA and plans to study for a Ph.D. –which she will complete in the next five years. In the meantime she will focus on bringing up her two daughters, and learning karate.

The founder and head of a respected local window-cleaning company, **Peter Simon** has announced his retirement with immediate effect. Over the course of the last 37 years he has overseen the company's growth from just two people (Mr Simon and his son, Albie) to one of the most respected companies in the area employing 14 people. Peter now plans to learn Russian to add to the French, Spanish and Italian in which he is already fluent.

STAGE 2: CHART YOUR POSITION

Next, you need to plot your current position. Below are some of the elements you might wish to consider:

▶ What does your day-to-day routine comprise?

▶ How much do you achieve in your work life?

▶ How do you spend your time outside of work?

▶ Where are you versus where you had hoped to be at this stage in your life?

Again, you need to be completely honest and truthful and as accurate as you can be. This list need be for your eyes only, so you are fooling no one but yourself if you pretend that you are far more productive than you really are. Equally, do not be tempted to understate your current productivity level just so that, further down the track when you revisit this chart, you can convince yourself that you are moving faster than you really are! A true and accurate picture of your real position at present may not make great reading straight after you have envisaged the future, but remember the whole point of this exercise is to determine the steps necessary in order to turn that vision into reality.

STAGE 3: PLOT YOUR COURSE

Next you need to plot the points in between these two extremes, and to determine any potential obstacles:

▶ How will you achieve your goals?

▶ What are the necessary steps to take you from your current position to where you want to be?

- What stepping-stones will you need to place to help you achieve this?

- Where will they be?

- Who will you need to get to help you and in what ways?

- What are the potential stumbling blocks and pitfalls along the way?

- What is preventing you from achieving your full potential?

- How might you increase your productivity?

- What is the timescale over which your plans are to be completed?

Now, you need to join the dots. You know where you are. You know where you want to be. You know the requisite steps along the way so know how you will achieve it. You know what assistance you will require and from whom, and you know the timescale for each. So you have everything you need to plot your course to maximum productivity and every reason to believe you can get there.

STAGE 4: BROADCAST YOUR FORECAST
Tell your friends, your family, put it on the Web – in fact, tell anyone who will listen. Shout it from the rooftops, because letting everyone know your targets is a great way of providing the incentive to achieve them. No one likes to fall short of their targets – everyone loathes doing so publicly.

Remember this: Publicizing Productivity Plans Powers Perfect Performance!

Remember this: Short-term obituaries

It can also be useful to write short-term obituaries. Write your year's, quarter's, month's, week's, and even day's obituary. What do you plan to have achieved by the close of play? How will you accomplish it? How will you measure your success? Then pin it on the wall, roll up your sleeves, and get to work.

Project management

Whether you have just one project on the go or already have several running concurrently, it is vitally important that you run each with precision and care. Inept project management is a sure-fire way to ensure that things are not accomplished in the best order to maximize your time and your productivity. Effective project management, on the other hand, allows you to see exactly when and how each stage of each process will be accomplished. By planning, organizing and managing your resources effectively you can combat the restraints of scope, time and budget to meet your project goals and objectives.

Motivation

'People who are unable to motivate themselves must be content with mediocrity, no matter how impressive their other talents.'

Andrew Carnegie

Achieving maximum productivity means working hard, and while the sense of achievement is consummately satisfying it's a good idea to give yourself a more tangible and immediate incentive for putting in the long hours and the hard graft. You also need to make it realistic. It is no good pretending that when you have achieved your goal you are going to buy yourself a new car if deep down you know it is never going to happen. Having long-term goals and even pipe dreams are an excellent idea – you just need to be clear that that is what they are.

You also need to give yourself something realistic to shoot for in the short and medium term, however – something you really will do or buy each time you reach a milestone (and if that happens to be a new car then so much the better). Or perhaps your long-term goal is to buy that car but your reward from increased productivity in the short term is a more modest half-day at the local go-kart track or a weekend away.

Whatever they are, ensure your goals are attainable and that they are not just hollow promises to yourself but that you actually do them when you achieve your goals. Looking back fondly on a great day out earned through your increased productivity is an excellent way of providing motivation for all future targets. And each time you feel your productivity waning you can revisit your proposed rewards to provide you with the necessary incentive to keep pushing yourself forward.

> 'People often say that motivation doesn't last. Well, neither does bathing – that's why we recommend it daily.'
>
> Zig Ziglar

Quick fix: Reward yourself

Spend a few minutes deciding what you would like your rewards to be. Not only is this very enjoyable but it also crystallizes what you're shooting for – providing immediate and tangible motivation.

Writing your goals and incentives into your productivity chart is a great way to keep them in mind all the time – and to provide a constant incentive. Let's have another look at Anna's productivity chart for redecorating her office:

	Week	Month	Quarter	Year	Ongoing
Completion date	May 7	June 1	July 31	April 30	
What do I want to achieve?	Tidy office	Paint office	Re-carpet and refurnish office	Have new office bedded-in	Keep office tidy
What are the likely barriers?	Lots of stuff which needs really sorting, not just moving	During redecoration: – Nowhere to store office items – Need somewhere else to work	Late delivery; storage; finding time to choose new furniture	Urge to keep re-arranging; keeping on buying additional furnishings; breakages; insufficient budget	Lack of time; too much 'stuff'; hoarding

(Continued)

	Week	Month	Quarter	Year	Ongoing
Coping strategies	Agree separate project for dealing with this	Agree with partner use of bedroom and living room as temporary store and workspace	Agree delivery and fitting in good time; accept deliveries only when office is ready for them; choose furniture at weekends	Be strict – get the arrangement right first time; only add to furnishings if really necessary; repair or replace as needed	Agree time to tidy – 10 minutes per day; keep accessories to a minimum; do not keep unnecessary items!
Reward	Bar of chocolate	New book	Meal out to celebrate	Magazine subscription	N/A
Am I on track...?					
Week ending 04/05	Yes – target achieved	Yes	Yes	Yes	N/A
Week ending 11/05	N/A	Yes	Yes	Yes	N/A
Week ending 18/05	N/A	No – not enough paint	Yes	Yes	N/A
Week ending 25/05	N/A	No – room requires extra coat of paint	No – carpet delivery delayed	No – 3-week delay	N/A
Week ending 01/06	N/A	No – target missed by 4 days	Yes – delivery back on track	Yes	N/A

Productivity chart – Project: redecorate the office

By creating, maintaining and completing your productivity chart for each project you will be able to see at a glance:

▶ What you plan to achieve.

▶ When you plan to have accomplished it.

▶ What the potential barriers are:

　▷ How you will overcome them.

　▷ How you will circumvent them.

- What reward you will give yourself upon successful and punctual completion.
- How you are doing at each and every stage.

This will enable you to set realistic targets, plan appropriately to meet them, and motivate yourself to do so – maximizing your productivity.

Remember this: Keep your productivity chart to hand

Make sure you maximize your productivity by keeping your productivity chart to hand at all times – and refer to it often.

Next step

In this chapter we have seen how careful planning and setting targets can be invaluable as you seek to boost your productivity. In the next chapter we will look at giving your daily routine a thorough overhaul.

7

Revolutionizing Your Daily Routine

In this chapter you will learn to:

▶ *Take regular breaks to boost your productivity*

▶ *Use your breaks to recharge and re-energize your mind and body, and to provide a real separation between work time and rest periods*

▶ *Maximize your commute to work and use this 'dead time' to increase your productivity*

▶ *Develop your own productivity plans, tailoring them to the needs of each piece of work as you go.*

How do you feel?

1 Are you able to make the most of every day? Of every hour?

2 Do you create plans which are optimized for harnessing maximum productivity?

3 Does working flat-out increase or diminish your productivity?

4 Do you use breaks as downtime or to more actively aid your productivity?

5 Do you utilize every aspect of your working day to increase your productivity?

Power productivity

In order to function at your most productive, you need to ensure that you are operating in the most energizing way possible. Continuous work without the opportunity to recharge both your mind and your body leads, over time, to a depletion in your ability to function at your maximum productivity. Equally, taking extended breaks will give you the opportunity to recharge but will cost you valuable time, which in turn will have a cost on your productivity. By scheduling regular, short breaks you can avoid the need to leave your work for extended periods while ensuring that you are functioning at your maximum. This is 'power productivity'.

The importance of regular breaks

Have you ever reached a point in your work at which you think you can't do a minute's more work without taking a break? That you are going round in circles because your head is so full you can't see the wood for the trees? That you are running on empty? If so you will have impaired your ability to be productive because the fact is that we all need to take regular breaks in order to work at our maximum potential. It's perhaps easiest when seen as an equation:

► 10 hours worked with steadily decreasing efficiency can be written as:

> 1 hour @ 100-per-cent efficiency
>
> + 1 hour @ 90-per-cent efficiency
>
> + 1 hour @ 80 per-cent efficiency
>
> + 1 hour @ 70-per-cent efficiency
>
> + 1 hour @ 60-per-cent efficiency
>
> + 1 hour @ 50-per-cent efficiency
>
> + 1 hour @ 40-per-cent efficiency
>
> + 1 hour @ 30-per-cent efficiency
>
> + 1 hour @ 20-per-cent efficiency
>
> + 1 hour @ 10-per-cent efficiency

= 10 hours @ a combined total of 550 per cent.

► Now divide the total productivity by the hours worked to see the average efficiency of the total time worked:

> 550 per cent/10 hours = 55-per-cent efficiency.

Clearly, working at little more than half maximum efficiency significantly impairs productivity.

► Now compare this to taking 10 minutes of every hour as a break which can be written as:

> 0.83.33 hours × 10 hours × 100-per-cent efficiency = a combined total of 833 per cent.

► Now divide the total productivity by the hours worked to see the average efficiency of the total time worked:

833 per cent/10 hours = 83.3-per-cent efficiency.

An increase in efficiency of more than 50 per cent!

And any increase in efficiency is by default an increase in productivity. And all this is achieved simply by taking regular active breaks – and while keeping your sanity! So even when you feel that you have so much to accomplish that you really cannot afford to take any breaks – indeed, especially when you feel you can't afford to take a break – you must discipline yourself to take a pause, step away from your work, and catch your breath.

But this time need not be wasted. It can and should be used productively to recharge your batteries and ensure that your work periods are used to maximum effect. One of the best ways to achieve this is to use the time to take some exercise, recharging your batteries both mentally and physically.

Active breaks versus passive breaks

If you use your breaks from your work simply to rest and relax, you may well find your mind still buzzing with the work you are trying to get away from, or worse still compiling a mental list of all the tasks which are still to be completed. By changing the breaks from 'passive breaks' to 'active breaks' and utilizing the time away from your desk to take some exercise, you will provide yourself with a positive reason for removing yourself from your work, both mentally and physically. You will also be injecting into your day some much-needed stimulus for your body and a complete break and genuine rest for your mind.

Most people who put in long hours at a desk job fall into the trap of thinking that they cannot afford the time to exercise. In fact, the truth is that you cannot afford *not* to take the time to exercise. It has long been held that a healthy body equals a healthy mind and if you want to keep your brain as active and agile as possible you could do a lot worse than keeping your body the same way – plus you'll be taking those all-important breaks from work and helping to keep your brain healthy and your outlook and your ideas fresh. So perhaps a better expression of what we need to achieve is:

An active body = an active, well-rested mind.

One of the simplest and most effective ways to accomplish this is to build it into your daily routine and discipline yourself to rigorously enforce it.

The 'power hour'

We have already seen that taking 10 minutes out of every hour to keep ourselves energized and mentally fresh can improve our productivity by more than 50 per cent. This works best if we try to get into the habit of never working longer than 50 minutes at a stretch and never breaking for longer than ten. This is the 'power hour' workplace routine and it is one of the most important things you can do to increase your productivity. Many people find that the easiest way to do this is to set an alarm to interrupt their work at the allotted time.

Case study

'My productivity increased exponentially the moment I bought myself an egg-timer for my office! I understood the principle behind taking regular breaks but was terrible at actually doing it. Often I would find two or three hours had gone by since I last took a break. The solution was to invest in an egg-timer which now sits in pride of place on my desk and alerts me without fail every time I am due a break. The difference has been remarkable and, given that it only cost £5, it is probably the most profitable business expense I have ever made!'

Quick fix: Buy an egg-timer

Buy an egg-timer for your desk, or set an alarm on your watch or phone, to remind yourself each time you need a break. Then make sure you actually take it! Don't fall into the trap of trying to complete the task you're on which will cause your all-important break to slide, or even disappear altogether.

However you choose to manage it, ensuring that you make the 'power hour' a staple of your work life will help you to reap rewards in a number of ways. Ten minutes may not seem like much time for a break but implemented every single hour without fail, and when used to take some brisk energizing exercise, it will:

▶ **blow away the cobwebs** of your current project

▶ help to give you **perspective** on your current work

- **release endorphins** to make you feel good
- get you **away from your desk** and provide you with a change of scene
- get you **out of the office** environment entirely if you so choose
- get your **blood pumping**
- give you a **mental break**
- give your batteries an **instant recharge**
- allow you to spend time getting **fitter instead of fatter**
- keep you **healthy**
- release **tension.**

Remember this: Get away from your desk

Sitting at your desk all day every day is a recipe for stagnation, both of your mind and of your body. So get up, get away from your desk and get exercising to breathe some new life into both.

You may find it odd at first taking an enforced break when perhaps you feel that you don't need one, or at a crucial juncture in a piece of work you are undertaking. You may certainly think it feels strange to spend 10 minutes of every hour of your work life exercising, and you may even think you cannot afford to devote some of your working day to keeping your body and your mind fit, but ask yourself this simple question – Can you afford not to? If you spend the majority of your working life sitting sedentary at a desk, then – although you want and need to be as productive as possible – you are in fact actively (or should that be inactively?!) constraining yourself in such a way as to make this virtually impossible.

The good news is that rectifying the situation does not require that you change into your gym gear, get into your car and head off for an hour's workout, followed by a shower, then another drive, all of which will probably take two hours and which you quite probably really do not have time for in the middle of your working day. And let's face it, while your boss will probably be sympathetic to you taking regular 10-minute breaks (they may not even notice!), they are unlikely to look kindly on a two-hour lunch break. Instead, all that is needed is 10 minutes each hour to devote to a workout – and, in fact, you do not even need to leave your desk to do it.

So you really have no excuse not to build regular exercise breaks into your daily routine, and just 10 minutes can make all the difference to how you feel, to your energy levels and your ability to give your best to your business and to maximize your productivity.

Myth-buster

A common misconception is that exercise is only worthwhile if you do it for a lengthy, sustained period. In fact, research has shown that engaging in **Maximum Intensity Training** (MIT) where you exercise as vigorously as possible can produce significant results with just three twenty-second bursts with short rests in between, undertaken three times per week. That's a total of just three minutes of exercise!

There are a plethora of published exercise routines which can help, one of the most famous being that by the Royal Canadian Air Force – 'Exercise Plans for Physical Fitness' – which describes an exercise system for 'shut-ins' (originally developed for pilots but just as good for anyone who works at a desk) comprising five basic exercises which are designed to work all the major muscle groups as well as the heart. Bear in mind that it is not designed to help you to lose a lot of weight or to train for a marathon but simply to retain a minimal level of cardiovascular and muscular fitness – and this is all that is required to boost your workplace productivity. The exercises can be completed at your desk since they only require a space approximately 1 metre by 2 metres and they are easy to remember and graded so that you can progress steadily. You can even do them when you are away on business trips since they take only 10 minutes, require no equipment and are designed so that you will not break into a sweat when you do them so you can crowbar them into even the busiest of days.

By finding just 10 minutes at a time to exercise, you can benefit from all the advantages, both mental and physical, of keeping active. Just make sure you get up and do it every 50 minutes using these quick energizers to relieve some stress, get your body active and your mind turbocharged. In this way, you can choose whichever exercise suits your mood at that precise moment, using them to provide convenient, frequent breaks throughout the day and thereby freeing your mind and spurring you to greater productivity.

'Walking is the best possible exercise. Habituate yourself to walk very fast.'

Thomas Jefferson

Another great way to keep fit and healthy is to invest in a **pedometer.** The recommended minimum number of steps you should take every day is 10,000 but how many of us really do? Try using the pedometer before implementing the 'power hour' workplace routine to see how many steps you really take on an average workday. Then turn every hour into a 'power hour' and use the 10-minute breaks to enjoy a brisk walk – you will almost certainly be amazed at the difference. Investing in a pedometer also provides a great fillip – it is wonderfully motivating to see how many steps you have taken in a day, what this equates to in miles/kilometres covered, and how many calories you have burned as a result. It also acts as a constant reminder to put in the effort to cover some more ground – even if it is just walking in circles around your office. Better still, if you can leave the office for a walk, you can get some fresh air while you burn calories and with a greatly reduced likelihood of getting dizzy!

> 'If it weren't for the fact that the TV set and the refrigerator are so far apart, some of us wouldn't get any exercise at all.'
> Joey Adams

Commuting

An inescapable part of modern working life for most people is the dreaded commute. However, with a little thought and consideration this can be put to good use. Of course, if your commute involves being somewhere where you can get on with your work (e.g. if you commute to work by train), then it is obvious how this time can be used productively. What is less apparent is how any 'dead time' can best be utilized to generate productivity in your working day. This may involve the majority of your commuting time (e.g. if you commute to work by car or if you walk or cycle to work), or it may account for just a small part of the commute (e.g. if you commute to work by train then it will be those portions of the journey which take you from your home to the train and from the train to your place of work – and vice versa). However much or little time is involved really doesn't matter. What does matter is how you utilize this time to ensure that your working day is as productive as possible and the most vital element of this occurs in your head.

The crucial task you will need to accomplish as you commute to work is making the **transition** from your home life to your work life. By ensuring that you arrive at work having shed all the trappings of home and enabling you to concentrate 100 per cent on your work you will be giving yourself every chance of maximizing your workplace productivity. By not doing so, not only will you be sharing your time between two things, instead of concentrating only on one, but you will be splitting your focus and impairing your ability to deal with all the issues which occur in your work since your mind will be slowed down by all the extraneous baggage you bring into your work life. So try to make sure that you use the commute, or at least a part of it, to mentally shake off your home life and blinker yourself so that you can concentrate completely on your work life.

Try to think of all the things in your home life which could have a negative effect on your working day – and then put them to one side. Very deliberately putting them in the 'Home Life' file in your head and putting them somewhere where they will not disturb you for the next eight or so hours while you work is a great way to clear your head of unwanted distractions allowing you to focus single-mindedly on the task at hand.

Next, order your thoughts for the working day ahead:

▶ What needs to be **accomplished**?

▶ By **when**?

▶ **What do you need to do** in order to make it happen?

▶ In what **order** should you tackle the various tasks?

▶ What is the **single most important thing** you need to accomplish today?

▶ What is the **very first thing** you should be getting on with the minute you get to the office?

Then keep this task at the front of your mind when you get to work and make sure you go directly to your office and do it. Also, be sure to make it something positive and proactive. Do not deliberately provide yourself an easy run-in with something like 'Check my emails,' or 'Look up that certain something on the Web I thought of yesterday that might, just possibly, one day, prove to be vaguely useful should a certain set of unlikely circumstances ever occur.' Instead, ensure that it is directly connected to the work you're doing and make it a definite task with a measurable outcome and a clear endpoint to slingshot you into your day.

> **Remember this:** Make the home–work transition
>
> No matter how long or short your commute it does not have to be unproductive. Used efficiently it provides you with an ideal opportunity to make the mental transition from 'home' to 'work', allowing you to make the most of your working day from the moment you arrive.

For those people who work from home, either full-time or part-time (an increasing number of people are opting to work from home not full-time but for a set number of days each week), there is an added complication – namely, that one of the great benefits about working from home is that you no longer have to face the dreaded twice-daily commute! Ironically, however, building a commute back into your working day might well be one of the most beneficial things you can do, providing an invaluable spur to your working life. The key reason for this is that it provides a physical and mental division between your home life and your work life giving you an endpoint to being 'at home' and a starting point to being 'at work', crucial if these physically occupy the same space. It is not actually a 'commute' at all, of course, but simply getting out of your house and 'arriving' at work is all that is needed to give you that all-important break.

Your commute need not be more than a 10-minute walk around the block to be beneficial; it just needs to be enough to create a clear demarcation point allowing you to mentally separate your home space from your work space and your home life from your work life. It will also afford you the opportunity to leave behind whatever baggage you may have in your home life (be it good or bad) so that you arrive at the office turbocharged and ready to go.

Productive planning

In order to maximize your productivity on any given project or task, you will need to plan in the most effective manner possible. But what is this? And does it change according to the needs of each situation? The first thing to understand is that productive planning works from the top down, creating a structure which will facilitate and define all the necessary elements within it – but that, crucially, it has the fluidity to enable you to respond to the changing demands of any given situation. The opposite of this, and the most detrimental to your productivity, is bottom-up or so-called 'reactive planning'. The truth, of course, is that there is no such thing as reactive planning! If you are reacting to a situation as it occurs, then you are not planning at all but firefighting – a method almost certain to guarantee that your productivity is minimized.

Imagine a situation in which, mid-project, something occurs which you had not foreseen and which needs to be reacted to quickly. The first thing that happens is usually a rush of adrenaline as anxiety or mild panic sets in. This is a situation which needs to be addressed, and addressed fast. So think quickly and decide immediately what needs to be done. Put it into action. Realize halfway through that it isn't going to work or that you have omitted something crucial. Quickly change course to accommodate this and keep driving forward – until you hit another roadblock, and then another and another and another … Without proper, productive planning this is a situation all too familiar, and it generates a sequence of events guaranteed to:

- **slow** you down
- **prevent you from achieving** the best possible result
- **obscure your thinking,** making further mistakes highly likely
- cause you real and unnecessary **stress**
- **blinker you** from seeing the bigger picture (e.g. what else needs to be done on this or other projects).

In other words, this is a method guaranteed to negatively impact on your productivity. There is a real danger in these situations that you will fall into the trap of thinking that the more you throw at the problem the quicker it will be resolved; or rather, not thinking about it at all but simply reacting on a gut-instinct level and hoping that this will solve the problem.

You may decide to throw more people at the problem in the hope that extra manpower will turn it around. You may decide to throw extra time at the problem, putting in extra hours in the mistaken belief that this is what is needed, when in fact all this does is tire you, making you less able to see what is really needed and further confusing the situation. You may be in a position to throw money at the problem, perhaps by bringing in external consultants or by bringing extra people onto your team from within the company; but all this does is slow you further by adding people who are unfamiliar with the situation and who may have completely new ideas (which can be a mixed blessing) but who will have to be brought up to speed first, which all takes time. And you may well find that their ideas are impractical or unworkable anyway. And all the while your team is getting bigger, less manageable, less efficient and making effective communication ever harder. In other words, your team is becoming less productive. What in effect you are doing is adding mass, when what you should be doing is adding clarity. The easiest way to see the differences between these planning methods is to see them in action.

A case study

Let us take as an example Roberta. She works in the public relations and press office of a large multinational corporation involved in the manufacture of building equipment and is undertaking a project of managing the organization and execution of a large outdoor event at which members of the public, dignitaries and specially invited guests will get to see her company's products at work.

REACTIVE PLANNING

Roberta decides to adopt the practice of reactive planning in the hope that by starting out with only sketchy details of what she hopes the final event will comprise she will be best placed to cope with as yet unknown circumstances as and when they arise. It is, of course, a mistaken belief and this heavily flawed approach leaves Roberta open to any number of incidences for which she will be woefully unprepared. By not having, from the outset, a very clear idea of what she will be doing and what she wants the eventual outcome to look like, Roberta is laying herself open to failure.

Imagine trying to build a house without detailed plans. You might start by building one large central room. Then, over a period of time, you might decide to add more rooms going off in different directions, a second floor, still more rooms all decided upon just before building them. Now imagine what the finished house will look like. From the outside it will in all probability look somewhat peculiar with an assortment of rooms of varying shapes and sizes protruding at all angles. However, the real failure of this approach will be seen only from the inside, and particularly when someone tries to live in it! Without a clear plan from the outset of the design of the house, let alone its construction, the unlucky occupants are certain to find that the layout is impractical as it has not been designed for comfortable living. In fact, the truth is that the house has not been designed at all, it has merely been built.

In the same way, Roberta's project is likely to end up as an uncomfortable mishmash of ideas, some of which may well have worked had they been properly implemented from the outset, others of which were never likely to work at all. As and when problems or opportunities occur, Roberta will find that far from being in an excellent position to cope with or benefit from them she is instead far too busy chasing her tail to take advantage of them. If she had had a proper plan from the outset, she would have been much better placed to deal with any problems and to take advantage of any opportunities which arose. Rather than having her eyes fixed only on the immediate issues, she would have been able to take advantage of a much broader perspective. This would have allowed her to:

▶ see **problems** well in advance and work out how best to deal with them

▶ see **opportunities** well in advance and work out how best to take advantage of them

▶ keep her eyes on **multiple issues** at the same time

▶ see and **take advantage of opportunities** which are not obvious and which would otherwise have passed her by (this is the planning equivalent of using your peripheral vision)

Remember this

Try to get into the habit of seeing projects from all angles.

Remember that you need to employ *funnel* vision not *tunnel* vision. So, by adopting the method of reactive planning, instead of creating a framework which allowed her maximum flexibility to deal with situations as they arose, what Roberta has really done is leave herself inadequately prepared. By having a clear idea of what you want the end result to look like you will have a clear vision for the project, which will in turn allow you to create a framework which will best enable you to get there. By starting without such a framework you are leaving yourself open to being dictated to by events as they occur since you will not have a firm foundation on which to build.

'Adventure is just bad planning.'

Roald Amundsen

Remember this

Proper Planning and Preparation Prevents Poor Performance.

RIGID PLANNING

Roberta decides that the best way to prepare for an event which is high profile, important to the company, and almost certain to be complex is to decide on a rigid and inflexible structure, and then stick to it. In this way, she hopes that her rigorous planning will ensure that there are no unforeseen eventualities which could throw the event off course. In this way, she hopes to maximize her productivity by investing all her time and energy into creating a robust plan which will not then need to be amended or altered. While her approach of detailed planning is to be applauded it has three major drawbacks:

1 No matter how rigorous Roberta is, it is completely impossible to foresee every potential eventuality.

2 By creating an inflexible planning structure Roberta is inadvertently creating the potential for disaster – if any unforeseen eventualities should arise (and they almost certainly will), she will be completely wrong-footed and unable to deal with them.

3 Roberta is investing all her time and effort in ensuring that her plan is 100 per cent robust meaning that she is devoting time and expending energy which will be wasted if the plan should start to unravel and require any adjustments.

The last of these points deserves particular attention. Typically 80 per cent of a plan will be completed in the first 50 per cent of the planning stage, and 95 per cent will have been completed within the first 70 per cent. The remaining 5 per cent of the planning will therefore take the remaining 30 per cent of the time. Given that the final 5 per cent will be very much dotting the *i*s and crossing the *t*s, trying to sort out the minutiae while all the major planning has already been accomplished, it is questionable as to how much worth can be placed in this final 5 per cent of the planning stage. Allocating almost a third of your time and effort to the sorting out and planning for the finest details (which may well have to be ditched anyway if any unforeseen circumstances should arise, which is highly likely) is seldom a productive way to progress. The question you will need to ask yourself is whether your resources could be better employed elsewhere – and the answer is almost always 'yes'.

So by creating a rigid and inflexible planning structure Roberta is effectively putting all her eggs in one basket, trusting in the hope that everything will go according to plan and that nothing unexpected will crop up at the last moment. In the best-case scenario everything will go according to plan and the event will be a success – but even in this case it is highly likely that Roberta will have unnecessarily wasted a lot of time, energy and resources. In the worst-case scenario the event will be a failure and Roberta will have wasted all her time, energy and resources.

What we need therefore is to find the most productive method of planning.

PRODUCTIVE PLANNING

Productive planning is efficient planning. As we have seen, an ad hoc, 'flying by the seat of your pants' approach in which planning is left to an absolute minimum or simply not invoked at all can lead to significant problems – the lack of a defined structure leaves the planner on a very unsure footing throughout. Equally, we have seen that attempting to plan for every last detail leaves the planner exposed to potential mishap as they will be completely unprepared to deal with any unforeseen eventualities as and when they arise.

The key to *effective* planning lies in the ability to create a sufficiently **robust structure** on which to hang all the elements of the project that the planner has every reason to be confident that the project will run smoothly, while at the same time building in a **degree of flexibility** so that as any unforeseen circumstances occur they will be well placed to deal with them. The most productive way of accomplishing this is by creating a rigid framework with definite points mapped along the way coupled with a flexibility of approach and implementation.

In our example Roberta is planning for a large outdoor event at which there will be a sizeable number of people, encompassing members of the public, dignitaries and industry insiders. She must therefore create a framework which allows for the needs of a mixture of attendees and also one which has the flexibility to cope with adverse weather conditions!

Taking this element alone we can see that if she were to adopt the **rigid planning model** Roberta would have to accept either:

▶ that things will quickly go badly wrong if the day doesn't provide the weather she was hoping for; *or*

▶ that she would have to create a minimum of two complete plans, and preferably more, to accommodate whatever weather the day might bring.

In the first of these Roberta is not so much planning as hoping for the best – hardly a productive way to carry on. In the second model she will be wasting a vast amount of resources, especially time and effort (but quite probably money too), in creating plans which ultimately will never be used. Again, not a productive model. Worse, she is following a path which *ensures* that she will be unproductive and leaves her no leeway to rectify it.

If, on the other hand, she were to adopt the **reactive planning model** Roberta would have to accept either:

▶ that she would need to alter her plans every time the long-range forecast changed; *or*

▶ that she would wait until the day and hope that she could change things as necessary in time – which is highly unlikely.

In the first of these Roberta is setting herself up for a nightmare two weeks preceding the event in which she will be flitting from one plan to another and another every time the wind changes – highly unproductive as most of her time and energy (and other resources) will be wasted. In the second Roberta is simply laying herself open to failure from the outset – the least productive model of all. And both of these examples are focused only on the weather – just imagine if you factor in all the other possibilities and imponderables how much ultimately unproductive planning you would have to do, or how much time, effort and money you would waste – or both.

So, in order to be productive with your planning, you need to approach it completely differently. You need to ensure that your plans and planning model are effective, ensuring that your time, energy and other resources are employed in the most productive manner possible. So how do you create a sufficiently robust structure on which to hang all the elements of the project while at the same time building in a sufficient degree of flexibility to allow you to accommodate any unforeseen circumstances as and when they occur?

We have established that the most productive way of accomplishing this is by creating a rigid framework with definite points mapped along the way coupled with a flexibility of approach and implementation – but what does this actually mean, in practical terms? And how do you go about it in order to maximize your productivity?

Creating a productive plan

The first thing you will need to do is to examine **what exactly the project will entail** and to envisage what you would like the **end result** to comprise. Only by having these firmly in mind are you in a position to create a framework which will enable it to happen. You will then need to plot all the points along the way, both in terms of those things which you will need to action and those things which you will require others to deliver (e.g. landmark points to be reached by your team, dates of delivery of supplies, work to be completed by external contractors or consultants, etc.).

Next, you will need to go through the entire plan highlighting all those areas which you have reason to believe may prove to be **problematic.** By identifying in advance all the potential pitfalls and pratfalls you are halfway to ensuring that they don't happen – and, if they do, you will be best placed to deal with them.

Now you need to go through your entire plan checking it for **fluidity.** This means ensuring that at each stage there is more than one answer to each problem and that if for whatever reason something should fail to materialise you already know how you will go about filling the gap.

Finally you need to revisit the entire plan ensuring that every step along the way is being **completed in the most productive way possible,** and that you identify ways of measuring this. This means being aware of such things as:

- time efficiency

- resource efficiency

- best use of external resources

- 'out-of-the-box' thinking

- fluidity of structure

- directness of route to project target

- measurement criteria.

The easiest way to keep on top of all this information is to create a chart which will enable you to keep track of your progress. Roberta's chart might look like this:

Date	What needs to be achieved?	How will I measure it?	Potential obstacles	Solutions to obstacles
01/01	• Project launch • Brief everyone on their roles • Convey project objectives	• Does everyone knows what their role is? • Does everyone have a clear vision of what we are aiming for?	• Breakdown in communication • Different visions of success	• Ensure all team members have written guidelines to follow • Periodically check that everyone is on side and on track
01/02	• Invites sent out • Replies received and noted • List continually updated • New invites sent to plug gaps	• Compile list of all invitees • Check for omissions • Ensure appropriate balance of public, dignitaries and industry insiders	• Lack of positive responses • Imbalance between target groups	• Include RSVP date – with sufficient time to issue new invites • Allocate one person to monitor the responses and issue new invites as a rolling programme
15/03	• Choose and book entertainment • Choose and book caterers • Choose and book staging supplier	• Will they provide what we require? • Can they do so within budget?	• Preferred supplier can't deliver to specification • Preferred supplier can't deliver within budget	• Need to compromise on requirements – or choose different supplier • Need to rejig budget to accommodate
31/03	Mid-project check	• Are we on schedule? • Are we on (or under) budget?	• Behind schedule • Over budget	• Determine cause and alter strategy • Recruit more people to team • Identify ways to scale back or save money • Get authorization for budget increase
01/05	• Staging being delivered	• Has everything ordered been supplied? • Is there anything not ordered now required?	• Unable to source missing components	• Have backup supplier readied in case of emergency

(Continued)

Date	What needs to be achieved?	How will I measure it?	Potential obstacles	Solutions to obstacles
18/05	• List of invitees finalized • Welcome packs put together for special guests	• Do the packs reflect both the event and the company? • Will they add value to the event?	• Fewer acceptances than expected will inflate cost per pack • More acceptances than expected will require more packs than initially ordered	• Build in flexibility of budget to allow for this • Ensure supplier can produce extra packs at short notice – if not, bring forward RSVP date
18/06	• Event today	• Did I achieve everything I planned to for the event?	• Running out of time • Going over budget	• Ensure that timescales are being met at each stage • Ensure that budget is on target at each stage

Over time it is highly likely that Roberta will add to this chart and amend it as necessary to reflect the changing situation. Indeed, she *must* do so – but she must remain aware of one thing throughout: altering the plan to accommodate changes is a necessary element of a successful, productive and organic plan – but it must never be used as a means to allow for errors to be smoothed out. If Roberta is exceeding her budget, she must look for ways to redress this by saving money elsewhere, and not simply increase her budget (although this should be in the plan as a last resort). If she realizes that the project is falling behind schedule Roberta must look for ways to increase the pace of the work – not simply look to alter the date of the event, etc.

Quick fix: Plan now!

This sort of plan can be created quickly and easily at any stage of a project. It will be just as useful if you're part way through a project as it would be at the outset, so don't wait until your next piece of work to draw up your plan – do it now!

Ultimately, then, plans which are truly productive are plans which combine the best of both worlds by creating a solid but flexible outline structure. The key elements of this are:

▶ that it has the capacity to bend to accommodate new challenges or opportunities as they arise;

▶ that it will absorb new challenges or opportunities without rupturing the framework;

▶ that it leaves you best placed to be able to take advantage of any opportunities the project brings;

▶ that it leaves you best placed to minimize any problems the project throws up.

Remember this: Minimal problems, maximum opportunities

By ensuring that the plan is robust and workable, you will have the confidence to deal with unexpected and unforeseen circumstances, and you will have created a framework which allows you the freedom to do so. Problems will be minimized and can be quickly dealt with while opportunities will be maximized and can be quickly taken advantage of.

Next step

In this chapter we have looked at three of the most powerful tools in your productivity arsenal – the 'power hour', 'transitioning' between home and work life, and productive planning. In the next chapter, we will look at how to keep a clear, cool head – even in the most challenging circumstances – and how to build and rebuild a productivity system.

8

Keeping a Clear Head and an Empty Inbox

In this chapter you will learn how to:

- *Create to-do lists which really work for you and review them often*
- *Simplify your work life to boost your productivity and to guard against being pulled in too many directions*
- *Begin each day with renewed productivity, making sure that you are mentally prepared for the demands of each day*
- *Select the productivity tools and techniques which work best for you and your situation*
- *Find out why productivity might lessen and try to rectify the situation as quickly as possible.*

How do you feel?

1 Do your to-do lists work the way you want and need them to do?

2 Do you wish you could simplify your work life?

3 Do you ever feel mentally clogged up?

4 Are your thoughts and processes ordered and structured to aid your productivity?

5 Do you have a robust 'productivity system' in place?

Structuring your thoughts for maximum productivity

One of the most common traps into which people fall when trying to structure their thoughts and become more organized, and thereby more productive, is thinking that, simply by writing down all the tasks which needs to get done, they are halfway to achieving them. The reality is that while it is essential to capture all the things which need to be accomplished so that:

▶ they do not get forgotten

▶ they are all in one place

▶ they can be structured and prioritized

the act of simply capturing them does not make them any closer to being accomplished! So, while it is undoubtedly a good idea to list everything as a logical and streamlined reference, it is important not to fall into the trap of thinking that simply writing them down is productive. It only becomes productive once you begin to action them. Indeed, there is a significant danger in compiling lists of this sort – namely, that putting them down on paper means they are out of your head and therefore no longer at the front of your mind, lulling you into a false sense of security and tempting you to take your eye off the ball.

It is therefore crucial to acknowledge that capturing in a list all the tasks which need to be accomplished is only a *first step*, and that it is only useful if you refer to the list, and refer to it often, and ensure that you are actually *doing* the things on your list. In this way, your list should, in the initial stages, get shorter as your productivity levels increase, and once you have achieved your maximum productivity you should find your list staying approximately the same length.

Remember this: Monitor your list

Keep an eye on your list, not only to monitor the tasks you need to accomplish but also to monitor its length. Although this will necessarily fluctuate as your workload increases and decreases periodically, it should always even up to about the same length over time. If you notice it getting longer and longer, then you know your productivity system is breaking down in one or more areas and that it is time for a review of your practices.

Another thing you must learn to do is to be ruthless with your decision-making for each and every new item which you are preparing to add to your list. Rather than simply include it because it has occurred and will no doubt need sorting at some stage, you should discipline yourself to go through the following workflow each and every time:

1 Determine whether or not it deserves a place in the list at all (it is amazing how many things don't but to which our knee-jerk reaction is to add them to a list anyway!).

2 If it does then you will have to determine its priority. This falls into two categories:

a **Importance**

▶ top priority

▶ important

▶ of secondary importance

▶ unimportant

▶ unnecessary

b Urgency

- extremely urgent – needs to get done today
- urgent – needs to get done this week
- pressing but not urgent – needs to get done this month
- of no urgency – needs to get done this year
- timescale unimportant – needs to get done at some point

When and only when you have determined whether or not a task deserves a place on the list at all, and if so where according to the importance of the task and the urgency with which it must be completed, should it be added to the list. By using this front-end approach to categorization you will ensure that your list comprises only tasks which genuinely need to be completed and that they are by default included in the list at the appropriate place. This will save you time and effort in having to prioritize the items in your list at a later date, will eradicate the need to continually re-evaluate the list, and will ensure that the list is always accurate and up to date.

The bare essentials

> 'Almost all quality improvement comes via simplification of design, manufacturing ... layout, processes, and procedures.'
> Tom Peters

While multitasking and prioritization are essential elements of modern work life, we are always more productive when we can simplify our tasks and pare things down to the basic essentials. By cutting out distractions we are better able to focus and improve our productivity and the quality of our output. Cutting out the 'white noise' of modern work life is an essential skill to master if we are to maximize productivity. To put it another way, every additional distraction – and by this I mean absolutely everything which is not your key focus but which demands your time and attention, even if it is itself work – is just one more thing getting in the way of your productivity.

If what you need to do is write an email then write the email and do only that. If you stop to write an email only then to answer the phone, reply to a message, answer a question or to deal with any of the myriad distractions with which we are continually bombarded in our modern work lives, then you are allowing yourself to be pulled in multiple directions, each of which is impairing your productivity. Try to think of your productivity as a finite resource – because essentially that is exactly what it is. Now picture every distraction and demand on your time and energy as taking up a fraction of that productivity. In this way, you can easily see that by allowing ourselves to be distracted, no matter how valid each distraction might be in its own right, we are laying ourselves open to a dramatic loss of productivity.

The psychology of maximizing your productivity

It is not sufficient simply to employ the productivity tools at your disposal and to learn and follow the recommended processes – you need to understand why these techniques work. And to do that you need to understand the psychology of maximizing your productivity. Since you are reading this book it is reasonable to assume that you are aware of the fact that there is scope in your life for improving your productivity, and that you are prepared to do something about it. The leap you now need to make in order for the tools provided in this book to be used as productively as possible is to make sure that productivity is at the centre of absolutely everything you do. It must become your mainstay, not just something which is tacked on, an afterthought; and it must be at the heart of all your processes, all your actions, and all your thoughts. This is because improving your productivity will enable you to become better at absolutely everything you do.

Think about it – Is there any area of your life where you would like to be *less* productive? Anything you do for which achieving less would be advantageous? Any element of your job in which you wish you could be less efficient or less capable? The answer is of course 'no', and by ensuring that productivity is at the centre of your approach in everything you do, you can make sure that you are as productive as possible in every area.

Remember this: Put productivity at the heart of everything you do

Try to get into the habit of thinking through everything you do in terms of its productivity, and try to get into the habit of doing this before you begin a project or piece of work – and then regularly during it. If you wait until a project is underway before you stop to consider its productivity you will already have lost valuable ground.

Clearing your 'mental inbox' every morning

One of the first things a lot of people do every morning upon arriving at work is to check their emails and voicemails and systematically go through them so that they can begin the day with an empty inbox. Apart from clearing any backlog so that they can start the day without feeling under the cosh, it gives them the opportunity to catch up with events and settle themselves into their day.

We have already looked at the merits and demerits of this approach to emails, voicemails, etc., but a great lesson can be drawn from this in respect of how we mentally deal with our productivity. By simply launching ourselves into our day without pause for thought in respect of our productivity, it is highly likely that we will wade in with an approach which is unproductive, or at least not as productive as it could be. By taking the time each day to begin by clearing your head of extraneous baggage and then thinking through your day and the tasks it will involve to gauge your approach and how productive it is, you can save yourself a lot of wasted time, effort and resources. In other words, you can help to safeguard your productivity.

Quick fix: More for less

Try thinking through your day from beginning to end, discarding any preconceptions or regard for old habits, and evaluate it purely from the aspect of productivity:

✳ Are you tackling the right things?

✳ Are you tackling them in the most productive order?

✳ Are you tackling them in the most productive manner?

✳ What do you need to do in order to improve your day's productivity?

And so on. By taking this methodical, systematic approach to boosting your productivity you can maximize your efforts and achieve more, for less.

Case study

'I used to arrive at my desk with a sinking heart and begin the slow and painful process of wading through all the correspondence which had found its way into my life overnight and accumulated on my PC and in my phone. This would always take about 45 minutes to sort through, even though most of it was just rubbish. Then I adopted the practice of getting my mind sorted for the day ahead first and suddenly I was getting through the same correspondence in 10 minutes. The difference? I knew what I needed to do and instead of reading everything and listening to all the messages I only bothered with a fraction of them – the others I just deleted straight away. And I'm not missing anything with this approach other than stress and time-wasting.'

Exfoliation for the brain!

Why is it that we so often look after our bodies but neglect to look after our brains? It is as if we just assume that the brain will look after itself, no matter what we throw at it or how much we (often inadvertently) abuse it. In extreme circumstances this can lead to a complete meltdown, and while this eventuality is extreme it is not at all uncommon. Even in less extreme circumstances not properly looking after our brains, our mental wellbeing, can lead to a massive disruption in our ability to be productive.

So just as you wouldn't neglect your body by not washing, so you must ensure that you take the time to look after your brain by giving yourself the time to 'clean' it – organizing your thoughts, getting rid of extraneous matter, purging the detritus and freeing yourself up to be as productive as possible. And just as you might take the time to periodically exfoliate your body, ridding it of dead skin cells to aid the regeneration process and allow the new cells to be seen and to properly function, so you should take the time to mentally exfoliate, ridding your brain of all the detritus which builds up there (often unnoticed and over a long period of time) and freeing it up to function at its maximum capacity.

The best way to achieve this is to follow the process described below, and to try to ensure that you do this as often as possible, but once per week as an absolute minimum. Ensure that you have at least 15 minutes of uninterrupted time ahead of you:

1 Find a quiet space away from your place of work.

2 Allow yourself to mentally get into 'neutral', not thinking about anything in particular.

3 Breathe deeply and allow yourself to relax.

4 Think through everything in your work life with which you are currently occupied.

5 Think through everything in your work life with which you will be occupied in the short to medium term.

6 Think through everything in your work life with which you will be occupied in the long term.

7 Bring to the front of your mind everything which is definitely necessary for your work.

8 Bring to the front of your mind everything which may be necessary for your work.

9 Bring to the front of your mind everything which is not necessary for your work.

10   Bring to the front of your mind everything which has been on your to-do list for more than a month and evaluate it – does it really need to be done?

11   Decide which items can be struck off your list.

12   Make the firm decision to permanently remove these items.

13   Picture them as words on a list, or as the tasks themselves (depending on whether you are a literary or image based thinker).

14   See them being removed and permanently deleted and add to them all those items which you identified in point 9. Try picturing them going into a rubbish bin and then the bin being emptied, or being put into a pile and setting light to them.

15   Relax in the knowledge that they have been permanently removed and picture the other tasks you previously identified filling the space they have left.

Your remaining tasks are now bigger in your mind, given more prominence and uncluttered by additional, extraneous items.

Mental 'dumping'

It is not sufficient to just think through your list of things you need to achieve, and by when, and then prioritize them and start working on them from the top down. The reason that this approach is insufficient is that it only goes part way to achieving what you need to achieve – a truly productive method of sorting and prioritization. There is an important element missing from this approach without which your brain will quickly become clogged and your ability to function at your maximum capacity will be impaired. This is hitting the mental 'Erase' button.

If you review your list and realize that some items just seem to stay on the list, always there and always dragging you down by reminding you that they need to get done but never moving up your list to actually get done since they never assume a sufficiently high priority, then erase them. The truth is that, if they haven't made it into the actionable section of your list over weeks or even months, then it's highly unlikely that they will ever get done. Allowing them to remain on the list is a sure-fire way of impairing your productivity since:

▶ they will never actually get done

▶ they will be a constant thorn in your side

▶ they will clog up your list making it too long to be properly manageable

▶ they will sporadically pull your focus from the things you really need to do

▶ they will still be on your list in a year's time, two years, three years...

And all the time they are on your list they are taking up a part of your resources, a part which could and should be put to much more productive use. Think of yourself as a computer. You have a finite capacity for storing information (long term) and a finite capacity for dealing with information and processes (short term). These are in effect your hard drive and your RAM. Now consider how important it is to periodically empty your computer's trash, to free up its resources so that it doesn't become clogged and overburdened. Failure to do this will lead to a slowing down of its operations and an impaired ability to function at its maximum capacity – in other words, impair its productivity.

So it is with your brain. Failure to properly manage your mental lists, and those long-term to-do lists which you commit to paper or screen, will impair your productivity by slowing your processes. And this is completely needless and avoidable. If something has been on your list for months (or even years!), then it's a pretty safe bet that it will never actually get done – but equally that it doesn't really need to get done at all. So delete it – from your lists and from your brain – and free yourself up to be as productive as you can be with the things which really matter.

Keeping your thoughts and your desk tidy

> 'I eat and drink at my desk, but I'm a tidy eater.'
>
> Jamie Zawinski

Most of us recognize the need for keeping our workstations as tidy as possible. Avoiding clutter allows us to see at a glance the things we have which are important, and also the things which we should have but which are missing. A tidy desk also puts us into the right frame of mind to work productively and helps to minimize distractions. So it is with our thoughts. If we allow our brains to become cluttered and our thoughts untidy it is all too easy to miss the elements which are important since we can't readily 'see' or access them.

Just as debilitating to our productivity is the fact that we can't see what is *missing*. And crucially, by allowing our thoughts to become disorganized and cluttered, we are putting ourselves into a situation where we are forcing on ourselves a state of mind which is completely unsuited to productive working. In other words, we are creating a mental state which does not allow us to be productive. By turning this situation around and ensuring that we order our thoughts and keep our minds 'tidy' we are giving ourselves the best possible chance of achieving maximum productivity through having an ordered, structured mind-set – crucial in the quest to maximize our productivity.

This can be done at any time and should be done frequently; you do not need to wait until a project is finished and a new one about to commence, or until you have plenty of time to devote to it. Ordering and structuring your thoughts can be accomplished quickly if it is done frequently since there will never be a large build up with which to deal. Try thinking of it as mental filing – if you leave it and leave it until you have a mountain of paperwork to sort through the task seems huge and will take a long time to accomplish. If you do it frequently, however, it will never take long and will take very little effort – but the rewards will be just as great. Also, you will have the benefits of being able to enjoy the benefits of ordered, structured thoughts all the time, not just as and when you get around to it.

EXERCISE: TIDY YOUR THOUGHTS – NOW!
Try ordering and structuring your thoughts right now – and then ensure that you keep it going on a regular, and frequent basis. With practice, you will find the approach which works best for you but the following will give you a good starting point until you have developed your own preferred method:

▶ Think through your thoughts and identify which elements are already ordered and structured and which are not.

▶ Concentrate only on those which are not and mentally label them so you know where they belong. For example, if they are **project-related**:

▷ Which project they are concerned with?

▷ Who else is connected to them?

▷ What are the timescales involved?

▶ If they are **not project-related** (e.g. IT, HR etc):

▷ With which department are they concerned?

▷ With which function are they concerned?

▷ With which person or people are they concerned?

- Classify each one according to its:
  - category
  - priority
  - timescale for completion.
- Decide where it fits in your mental filing system.
- Mentally put it in the correct place and make the firm decision to leave it there until or unless it really needs to be moved.
- Revisit this process as often as possible.

Your productivity system

It is important not to see each component of what makes you more productive in isolation but rather to see them as separate pieces which together form one large system. This is your 'productivity system' and comprises all the techniques and tools which you use to help you to operate at your maximum productivity. As with any system, it is important to make sure that each component is functioning the way you need it to be, and to identify any aspects which are not working for you, and to revise and adjust them as necessary. In this way, you can be sure that your system for achieving maximum productivity is supporting you in all aspects of your work life, all of the time.

Myth-buster

It would be easy to fall into the trap of thinking that, once you have put into practice the techniques and tools in this book, your productivity will be permanently boosted. The fact is that, in order to ensure that you are functioning at your maximum productivity all of the time, you will need to review and revise your productivity system on a regular basis. You may find that some elements aren't working in the way that you had hoped, or that others which you thought weren't for you will actually be extremely beneficial. And we all fall into bad habits over time and become lax in our discipline in implementing our productivity system, so checking that it is working as well as it can be – and that it is working for you in the way that you need it to be – is important in the quest to keep your productivity at 100 per cent all of the time.

REVIEWING AND REVISING YOUR PRODUCTIVITY SYSTEM

In order to ensure that you are functioning at your most productive all the time you will need to implement a process for reviewing your productivity and measuring its effectiveness. This could be as simple as making sure that you are content with the amount you are achieving or it could involve a full 'systems check' of everything you do. This is very much a personal choice and you will need to find what works best for you, but it is important to make sure that you review your productivity on a regular basis to see:

▶ if it is working as **effectively** as it could be

▶ if it is working in the way **you** need it to

▶ if there are any elements which are **not working effectively**

▶ if there are any elements which are **not working at all**

▶ what you can do to **improve** the system

▶ what you will need to do to rectify any **major faults** in the system.

By reviewing your productivity system on a regular basis you will give yourself the best possible chance of maintaining your productivity at its maximum capacity most, if not all of the time. This is because:

▶ you will catch any **breakdowns** in the system at an early stage

▶ you will be able to see what is **working well for you** and use these elements elsewhere in your system

▶ you will be able to **identify any gaps** in the system and rectify them

▶ you will **not waste valuable time** operating with a productivity system which is not as robust or as helpful as it could be.

Regular 'systems checks' are therefore very beneficial and can save a lot of wasted time, energy and resources. As the old adage states, 'A stitch in time saves nine' and catching any faults early will help you to ensure that you are always operating at your maximum productivity potential. So try to get into the habit of reviewing your system regularly, and frequently.

> 'To improve is to change; to be perfect is to change often.'
> Winston Churchill

Quick fix: Get proactive

One school of thought maintains that: 'If it ain't broke, don't fix it.' In other words, just checking your productivity system for flaws is all that is required. Another, more proactive school of thought, however, maintains that 'Nothing was ever hurt by being improved'! So try to get into the habit of implementing regular checks and not being content with simply fixing any errors or filling any gaps but actively looking for ways in which you can better tailor the system to your needs and improve its overall efficacy.

ENVISAGING THE 'WHAT IF?' SCENARIOS – AND DEVISING COPING STRATEGIES TO DEAL WITH THEM

In a perfect world nothing would ever go wrong with your productivity system or in any way impair your ability to function at 100 per cent of your productivity potential all of the time. But then, if we lived in a perfect world, you wouldn't need to boost your productivity in the first place! It is much better, then, to adopt a realistic attitude and approach and by accepting that things may well go wrong from time to time you can be as prepared as possible to deal with any problems with which you are beset:

1 The first thing to do is to try to identify those areas in which there may be a **weakness** or which present **the greatest opportunity for setbacks.**

2 You will then need to identify those areas in which any setbacks would be most **damaging,** even if they are less likely to occur.

3 Lastly, you will need to identify a **coping mechanism** for dealing with each one. Use the following table as a starting point and adapt it as necessary to suit your needs and your situation.

'What if...?' scenario	Coping strategy
You are not achieving as much each day as you would expect	Are your expectations realistic? If so, check your productivity processes: • Are they sufficiently robust? • Do they cover all necessary areas? • Are they being implemented all the time?
You are not achieving as much each week/month as you would expect	Are your expectations realistic? If so, check your productivity processes: • Are any areas being overlooked? • Are the processes being implemented sufficiently frequently? • Do they maintain productivity over a sustained period? • Do you need to implement any additional processes or checks?
Projects are taking longer than you would expect or are producing inferior results	Are your expectations realistic? If so, check your productivity processes: • Are they sufficiently robust? • Are there any gaps? • Are they being monitored regularly? • Are there any which need to be implemented more frequently?
You are not achieving the quality of output you would expect	Are your expectations realistic? If so, check your productivity processes: • Are they appropriate to your needs? • Are they appropriate to the needs of the project? • Are they being rigorously implemented? • Are they being reviewed sufficiently frequently? • What else might you need to implement to address any shortfalls?

You don't need to wait until a 'suitable moment' to construct a 'What if...?' scenarios list. This is because:

▶ it only takes a few minutes to begin your list

▶ you do not need to complete your list in one sitting – it is best if it is allowed to grow organically over time

▶ there will never be a 'suitable moment' – the right time is now!

When it comes to envisaging roadblocks and challenging situations which might impair the productivity you've worked so hard to achieve, there really is no point in delaying the inevitable. It must be done and the sooner the better – after all, forewarned is forearmed and you can never, ever be too prepared.

When less is more

While there is no such thing as being too productive (as opposed to over-productivity – simply producing too much), too prepared or too well planned, it is possible to spend too much time on planning to try to boost your productivity – to the detriment of actually getting on with projects in which you can be productive. In other words, you need to determine which processes, techniques and tools are right for you and develop your own bespoke productivity system – then get on with implementing it. If you spend too much time trying to create and refine, then further refine and adjust and tweak and hone and polish the perfect system, you are in danger of impairing your productivity simply by trying too hard to boost it!

So it's important to realize when you start out that you need to limit the amount of time you spend planning to be productive since the only way you will ever actually be productive is to **stop planning and start doing.** In any case, you will only really know what works for you and which tools are going to be the most useful for you by field-testing them. Also, your system should evolve over time and even change according to your needs on any given project, so there really is very little benefit in attempting to create the perfect system prior to implementation. Just remember to review and revise your system as you go along.

Fantastic productivity systems aren't built, they're *re*built. In order to maximize the efficacy of your productivity system, you will need to combine periods of building it with periods of testing it 'in action' and periods of review and revision. Then go back to the building stage and rebuild it, deconstructing, removing, adding and fine-tuning as necessary. It is this combination used in continual rotation which will give you the best chance of developing the best system for you and your needs (even if those change over time or with each project).

For the very best results you should try to ensure that this is a never-ending process – but that doesn't mean it needs to take for ever! Revisiting it often for minor revisions is usually the best approach, and the easiest to implement.

Remember this: An ongoing process

It is highly unlikely that you will get it right first time. It will take time to fine-tune your productivity system and this will be an ongoing process so be prepared to keep updating it and adjusting as necessary.

Next step

Having mastered the art of building and rebuilding our productivity system, it's now time to focus on that foundational tool of modern working life – information technology.

Productive Use of Information Technology

In this chapter you will learn how to:

▶ *Determine the IT tools which are best going to serve you*

▶ *Keep connected in ways and at times which suit you*

▶ *Master the art of free-flowing communication without interruptions*

▶ *Manage your information productively, use the best management lists for your situation*

▶ *Safeguard your data – put robust safeguards in place for long-term data storage.*

How do you feel?

1 Do you utilize information technology tools to best advantage to boost your productivity?

2 Do you feel overwhelmed by the array on offer?

3 Are you using the most suitable tools for your situation?

4 Are you connected to and communicating with colleagues, clients and customers in the most productive possible manner?

5 Is your long-term information stored securely, or are you at risk of a crippling data loss?

Is the increasingly sophisticated information technology at our disposal the answer to our prayers, or a nightmare adding yet more layers of complexity to an already challenging situation? Is it an easy way to boost our productivity or an unnecessary distraction likely to slow us down and hinder our productivity? The answer, of course, is that it can be both of these, and often both at once.

Used in the right way IT can be both labour- and time-saving and can help us achieve a level of productivity which would be unimaginable without it. It can help us to organize, create, communicate, illustrate, demonstrate and a host of other things which modern work practices demand, and to do so with skill, precision and relative ease. Used incorrectly, however, it can all too easily get in the way of our productivity by slowing us down and creating completely avoidable roadblocks.

One fact is undeniable, however – information technology, instant communications systems, social media, etc. are here to stay and will only become more and more important to modern working practices as time moves on, so not getting to grips with them and learning how to use them to boost productivity is a sure-fire way of leaving yourself behind.

Used efficiently, IT really can help to maximize productivity – for example, it can:

- ▶ facilitate fast communications

- ▶ allow communication to multiple sources at once

- ▶ keep an infinite number of people informed on any subject

- ▶ aid efficient organization

- ▶ help you to keep in touch with colleagues, customers, clients, etc.

- ▶ facilitate expedient management of data

- ▶ create interest in products, technologies, research, etc.

- ▶ allow instant sharing of information across a number of media

- ▶ help to keep you and your work front of mind for customers, clients, colleagues, etc.

Since the technologies available to you have the capacity both to aid and to hinder your productivity, you can see that it is not the technologies themselves which create the problem or provide the solution but our *use* of them. With so much choice on offer, it is vital that you work out which of the myriad technologies available will boost your productivity, which are fun to use but don't actually add to your ability to be productive, and which will actively impair your productivity.

> 'Information technology and business are becoming inextricably interwoven. I don't think anybody can talk meaningfully about one without the talking about the other.'
>
> Bill Gates

Remember this: Review your IT tools

Used appropriately, the tools at your disposal can considerably boost your productivity but they also have the capacity to impair it. Try to find the time to periodically review the tools you use to ascertain which are working well for you and boosting your productivity and which are hindering you by impairing your productivity, and make adjustments as necessary.

Maximizing your productivity through the application of information technology

Information technology and the associated technologies of communication and connectivity may be things which inspire and excite you or they may make your blood run cold; either way, these are a fact of modern working practices. What is more they are becoming increasingly important and increasingly sophisticated creating two conflicting possibilities:

1 Their ability to **help** you in your work has never been greater.

2 Their ability to **hinder** you in your work has never been greater.

In order to make an informed choice about which of the many tools available to you will assist you and boost your productivity, and which will do the opposite, you will need to have a thorough understanding of:

► what each does

► how they work

► how you can use them

► what functions they will fulfil

► how they are used by others

► how they would fit into your work life

► how they would help to boost your productivity.

The technologies and tools you will need to consider can be broken down into four main areas: information, communication, connectivity and data management.

INFORMATION

Thanks to the Internet, there has never been an easier time to research and gather information. By accessing the World Wide Web, be it from a computer in the office, a wireless-enabled laptop in a 'hotspot' (an area which provides remote

Internet access, often free of charge) or from a mobile phone or similar device with sufficiently fast data download capability (usually 3G or better), we can instantly plug into a world of information accessed through powerful and increasingly accurate search engines (such as Google, Yahoo, Ask, etc.). And having the world's largest and surely most comprehensive encyclopedia, Wikipedia, never more than a few clicks away can certainly save an awful lot of time when compared to the methods of choice previously at our disposal such as going to a library or bouncing from one phone call to the next trying to get closer and closer to that elusive piece information. Just bear in mind that, because content is uploaded by users all around the world, Wikipedia is open to a degree of inaccuracy, although by and large it tends to be pretty good.

Another word of caution – the World Wide Web can be dangerously addictive and 'surfing' (skipping contentedly from one website to another, tangential and equally tempting, site, or on to a different type of site altogether sparked by a reference or recommendation) can cost countless working hours if you are not wise to the risk and careful to be very disciplined.

> 'Anyone who has lost track of time when using a computer knows the propensity to dream, the urge to make dreams come true and the tendency to miss lunch.'
>
> Tim Berners-Lee

In terms of productivity, we can perhaps replace 'lunch' with 'opportunities'. Tempting as it may be to surf the Web, since there will almost certainly be things which interest you which have been uploaded by someone somewhere, it has the propensity to have a profoundly negative effect in terms of productivity. Any time spent idly, albeit enjoyably, surfing the Web is time you're not spending on the work you should be doing, costing you not only the time you spend surfing but also the time it takes to readjust and get back into the frame of mind to continue with your work. Moreover, such distractions have an alarming tendency to multiply without any effort on your part and often without you even noticing!

There is a good reason why most companies restrict their employees Internet access at work and block the use of certain sites (particularly social media, unless they are specifically needed for work purposes). Whether or not this is done in your situation, you should establish your own rules for Internet use so as to ensure your productivity is enhanced and not restricted by this unquestionably beneficial tool.

Quick fix

Define and implement your own Internet rules of engagement!

Used appropriately, however, the Internet can be an invaluable productivity tool and the ability to access information and resource materials instantly and with such ease can save countless hours and circumvent a good deal of stress, both of which are crucial in the quest for maximizing your productivity.

Remember this: A double-edged sword

The World Wide Web is one of the most valuable and productive resources available to you and your work, but is also one of the most addictive, alluring and potentially dangerous to your productivity.

Communication

Like it or not, we are in the age of continuous and never-ending contact, and this is something which is increasingly being expected and demanded by clients, customers, suppliers and even colleagues. As we have seen in earlier chapters, however, such contact can often hinder us more than it helps, so two simple ground rules need to be established in order to ensure that your workplace productivity is not compromised:

1 Any and all **non-work-related communication** must be eschewed during working hours – and that includes any

time spent working, whether in the office, on the road or from home.

2 **Work-related communications** should ideally be left until they can be dealt with as a batch. Where this is not possible, try to restrict those communications you allow only to those which relate directly to your current project. Do not get sucked into the mire of responding to communications about future projects, past projects, or even projects on which you are not and will not be involved, during those periods of your working day when in order to be most productive you need to be fully focused.

Case study

'My productivity took a nose-dive when I went freelance because suddenly everything was available to me all the time. I was so excited and found it so liberating to make my own rules and set my own standards that I took far too many liberties, although at the time I didn't really realize it. The opportunity to phone my friends whenever I wanted to, for instance, was far too tempting to ignore! Also, they knew about my new-found freedom, and now that I had left my employer where taking social calls during business hours was a strict no-no they were free to phone me whenever they wanted to. The biggest time-wasters though were Facebook and Twitter, where I would spend half an hour at a time frequently throughout the day, catching up on what my friends were doing and posting about my life.

'At first, it was wonderful until I took stock of my situation and realized that I hadn't achieved nearly as much as I had expected to. Not only was I spending too much time on the phone and on social media sites but, more damaging to my business, potential clients were being put off by the way I was never available. Of course, I only realized this with hindsight and made moves immediately to remedy the situation – including risking hurting my friends by telling them they could no longer call me during office hours and not responding to messages posted (in fact, not even checking them). As soon as I made the change two things happened – I felt freer and my productivity soared. A valuable lesson.'

Connectivity

Connectivity tools can help to keep you connected to your business, your suppliers, your clients and even your colleagues, and as such they can be very helpful by allowing you to keep track of demands, get a feel for what is going on in your market, stay one step ahead of the game, and generally stay connected at all times with a minimum of effort. We have looked at communication as a separate topic because it is such a vital and wide-ranging area even though it could be broadly grouped under the heading of 'Connectivity'.

Connectivity in a larger sense, then, is all the other methods we have at our disposal for keeping connected to our working life, to our customers, clients, colleagues and even competitors whenever and wherever we may happen to be, and allowing, indeed encouraging, *them* to keep connected to us. Facilitating this is fundamentally important to fostering a good and long-lasting relationship and it can be a great way of allowing people to stay interested in what we do through passive, non-invasive communication.

The danger, however, is much the same danger as is prevalent with communication technologies; namely that, unless you are very strict about what you do and do not allow into your work life, and how you manage it, you can all too quickly become embroiled in the many Internet-based connectivity tools at your disposal. Unless you are very careful to ensure you use only those which have a positive impact on your work and to determine when and how you will use them, you can quickly find that they are impairing your ability to be productive, and far from helping your business they are hindering it.

Your job, therefore, is to ensure you have provided sufficient tools to enable this to happen and made them sufficiently accessible and user-friendly that they are easy and enjoyable to use without stretching yourself too far – certainly, you must not employ tools whose management requirements will be such that tending to them impacts on your ability to be productive. You will also need to make sure that everyone knows about them and that they are kept relevant through regular updates.

Employed appropriately and carefully managed, these connectivity tools can actively aid your productivity since they can:

▶ **free up your time** by keeping you in touch with clients, customers, colleagues, etc. without the need for you to be hands-on

▶ allow you to **determine when you will respond** to direct communications

▶ facilitate your ability to deal with **batches of communications in one go,** thereby avoiding the need to deal with them piecemeal

▶ allow you to **keep your finger on the pulse** of your work area

▶ keep the **channels of communication open** constantly and continually.

With the number of different methods available today we are spoilt for choice, with a wide range of styles and varying degrees of technical expertise required by the user. As a general rule, it is better to employ only one very well-designed and targeted tool than to try to cover all bases and overstretch yourself. Most importantly of all, try to ensure that you use those types which will not *cost* you time but will instead help to *free up* your time. In this way, they can be a godsend, automatically boosting your productivity with little or no extra effort on your part.

While it may be tempting to want to encompass every tool at your disposal, either because you feel that you are missing out (on work, communications, keeping ahead of the curve, etc.) or because you are unsure which will prove most useful, this will take a good degree of time and effort and will therefore hinder your productivity even if some of the tools are working well for you. It may therefore be advisable to try several in turn to see which work best for you. Try to determine:

▶ which are **quickest and easiest** for you to use

▶ which **provide most closely what you need**

▶ which best project the **image** that you wish to convey

▶ which are most likely to be favoured by **those you wish to use them** (and therefore more likely to be used)

▶ which provide you with the **maximum flexibility** in approach and implementation

▶ which are overall most likely to help you to **maximize your productivity.**

In this way, you can get a clearer idea of where you should focus your time and resources, both of which are all too easily stretched in today's fast-paced business world. Do not forget that you can always add more at a future date, and even take offline any which are not working for you. Just bear in mind that if you do take any offline you will need to ensure that:

▶ you **take with you** any current users

▶ you are as certain as you can be that **you will not need them in the future**

▶ you give users **plenty of notice** and opportunity to begin using the tools you are sticking with

▶ you will not unnecessarily **lose goodwill** by doing so or **create problems** for your users.

It is, of course, highly probable that you will not get it right first time, so get into the habit of monitoring the usage of any connectivity tools in which you invest and asking your clients, customers and colleagues if they have tried them yet and, if so, what did they think. Then use this valuable feedback to help tailor the tools you use in future – and remember to keep checking that what you are providing is what is wanted.

Quick fix: Get specific feedback

In order to get the most useful feedback from your clients, customers and colleagues on your connectivity tools, try to structure your questions in an open manner so that you gain real insight. Do not just ask them whether or not they thought the tools were good – ask specific questions such as what were their favourite and least favourite aspects of the tools, which they used for longest and why, and what they would like to see in the future.

Some of the more commonly employed connectivity tools which can help you to maximize your productivity by facilitating your ability to keep in touch with your colleagues, customers and clients include Facebook, Twitter, YouTube and blogging, and each will have their own merits and demerits with regard to your particular work area and therefore your business productivity. Look at each in turn to determine the best place to focus your efforts.

Remember this: Business, not pleasure!

Ensure that whichever connectivity tools you employ you use only for business connectivity – never ever allow yourself to use them for personal use during work time or your productivity will almost certainly suffer, and suffer badly.

FACEBOOK

Many companies are now turning to Facebook as a method of communicating with their audience. One of the advantages this affords is that the communication is two-way, enabling visitors to keep updated with the latest information on your company and your offer while at the same time providing them with the means of contacting you to provide feedback, ask questions and so on. Another is that it is free of charge!

A further string to Facebook's bow is that it is primarily a social networking medium so a company's page can leverage this equity – visitors are likely to be less guarded and less sceptical when reading a Facebook page than when visiting a company's website. However, as it is primarily a social networking tool it is not specifically tailored to the needs of the business user, so you will need to consider exactly how it can best be employed to facilitate the connectivity and communication which will aid you in your work life. You will also need to be careful not to abuse the trust with which your visitors read your page so as to not appear cynical.

Quick fix: Focus on your goal

Try to determine whether using one of the connectivity tools at your disposal is the best way to achieve your aims. There may be a quicker, easier and simpler way of doing the same thing. Rather than asking yourself how you can benefit from using the tools, try asking yourself what it is you hope to achieve and then see whether these tools are the best way of doing it.

TWITTER

This is a form of mini blog used mainly for social commentary but it can be a useful way of keeping people updated on a very regular basis for businesses, too. This is particularly useful as a sort of pre-emptive strike if it means that by doing so you are forestalling the need for other people to communicate with you requesting situation updates, frequent and brief project reports, etc. By posting messages, known as 'tweeting', you can ensure that you are doing so at a time of your choosing, thereby safeguarding your productivity by ensuring that you are not subject to a stream of constant interruptions.

If you are using it to update clients or customers rather than colleagues, you will need to update it very frequently (preferably at least once per day) in order to keep it relevant and this is not only time-consuming but requires that your subject has no end of talking points which your potential audience will find interesting and stimulating. If this is appropriate to your work, however, it can be a great way of keeping the channels of communication open and fast-flowing. In order to ensure that it is aiding your productivity and not hindering it, you will need to be clear about:

▶ how **necessary** such communications are

▶ whether this is the **best and most practical** means of providing the information to your audience

► whether you need – and intend – to communicate in this way on a **long-term basis**.

Remember this: Tweeting is high maintenance

Tweeting can be a great way of keeping clients posted on all your business activities and can actively aid your productivity by keeping you in control of your communications strategy – but it is very high maintenance. Before you begin, therefore, you will need to be clear about your reasons for wanting to maintain such regular contact and your ability to do so.

If you decide that this is the connectivity tool most beneficial to your situation, then you will have the freedom to use it anywhere since it can be used from a large number of mobile platforms as well as desktop workstations. One of its real advantages is that every message you post is strictly limited to a maximum of 140 characters. This not only ensures that your time is not too badly eaten into but ensures that you focus your message on what you want to say. Since there is no room for waffling, you will need to be concise, condensing your message and thereby increasing its impact.

Try it now: Write a tweet

If you want to know whether this punchy style of communicating is going to work for you, try thinking of something you might want to tell your audience and then commit it to paper or screen in 140 characters or fewer. Don't forget that punctuation and even spaces count toward your total, so really try to pare it down. If you find it difficult at first try:

* thinking about the **essence** of what you want to say and saying only that
* substituting long words for **shorter** ones
* **rewriting** phrases and sentences with **brevity** in mind
* using **abbreviations** where possible
* keeping it **punchy** – don't worry about the flow of sentences
* thinking of it as **distilling** your message, leaving only the important bits and saying them as clearly and strongly as possible.

In a business context, tweeting is perhaps most useful if you need to maintain a constant connection with your clients to keep your business permanently front of mind and it will need to be in a tone and style which is entertaining. In other words, you need to give your customers a reason to want to keep checking back. It is free of charge to use but remember that this is not a one-to-one tool but a means of communicating quickly and easily with a wider audience so all your tweets must reflect this in tone, style and content.

Remember this: Warning!

Because your tweets can be read by anyone who wants to follow what you say, you must be extremely careful not to post anything of a private nature or which you wouldn't want everyone to read. There have been some famous, and highly embarrassing, instances where this was not the case.

YOUTUBE

This hugely popular video broadcast website is a great way to provide video content to your clients. A simple link on your website can connect them straight to this material, with the added benefit that YouTube users might enjoy your videos and then search out your website on the Internet. The main point to consider here is whether or not you have any material which is suited to this form of communication – if it would be better served just by being on your website, then you should limit it to that.

The real benefit in terms of productivity is that it enables you to reach an entirely new audience, one which might not necessarily visit your website. So if your business is of the ilk that such communication is beneficial, then this can be a real time-saver, making it a great addition to your arsenal of productivity-enhancing tools.

BLOGS

Another option you may wish to consider is a blog. This is simply an online spiel about whatever you want it to be about – updates about your company, musings on the state of the industry, thoughts on the latest trends, or reviews of anything you might use in your business etc. Quite simply, there are blogs about anything and everything. As with the other connectivity tools we have looked at, if blogging is to boost your productivity you will need to ensure that:

- there is a **real need** to communicate with your audience in this way

- you have the **time and inclination** to sustain it (otherwise it can quickly have a negative impact on your productivity)

- your **productivity really will be aided** by blogging.

If you determine that blogging will indeed be an effective tool for what you need to accomplish, then there are a number of providers whose sites you can use to get you started. The key, so often ignored, is to keep your blog **focused** and regularly updated to keep it **relevant**.

▶ Focus

All too often a well-meaning business blogger gets sidetracked and either starts to discuss something of interest to them but unconnected to their business (and so unlikely to be of interest to their readers) or to use their virtual soapbox to rant and rave and generally vent their spleen about any number of ills which ail their business and patently are not their fault!

Either way this is unproductive, as it merely creates a distraction and wastes valuable time. Others use it as a virtual pulpit from which to preach worthily about business matters or just life in general, all of which might make them feel better but are unlikely to do much to boost their productivity. So try to keep your blog focused on your business – it can be useful to get someone else to review it from time to time to make sure that it stays on track.

▶ Relevance

By updating your blog regularly and frequently, you ensure that the content is always topical and relevant, and you provide a reason for your customers to visit your site on a regular basis, so try to get into the habit of updating your blog at least once per week, and updating it at approximately the same time and on the same day (or days) each week.

By getting into a routine for managing the content of your blog you can maximize your productivity since it will take less time and less effort than if you were to do it piecemeal.

This also ensures that your website looks modern and cared for and your business appears up to date and together. If you visit a website with a blog which has not been updated for weeks (or months or years), it does not fill you with confidence about the company – and is very telling about the productivity of the blogger! So, if you are going to blog then make sure that you blog regularly and ensure that your topic is one about which you are passionate and have plenty to say.

Remember this: To blog or not to blog?

It is better not to blog at all than to blog poorly, and once you have started a blog it may be damaging if it is not updated regularly or if it suddenly disappears altogether. It is easy to start a blog but it can be difficult to maintain it, and if you start to find that it is taking more and more time and becoming more and more of an effort to keep it going then you will need to re-evaluate its worth to your business life and assess whether it really is aiding or hindering your productivity.

If you decide that it is worthwhile keeping it going, then take the necessary steps to make it work for you; if you decide that it is not, then close it down over a period of time and only after giving your followers plenty of warning – and plenty of information about where they can find out about your work instead.

Which technologies are right for you?

It is impossible to cover all the different communication and connectivity tools at your disposal without devoting the entire book to it – and quite possibly not even then! And, as technology evolves, the choices change and the spectrum widens. So how can you best go about choosing which tools to employ? The quickest and easiest way is to complete a table such as the one below which allows you to identify your needs, what might help meet them and how it can be reviewed:

What do I need to achieve?	Which tools can help?	How much time will they take?	How much effort will they take?	How will I measure the results?	How can I quantify the results?
Regularly update audience on project progress	Twitter	A few minutes, several times per day	Significant – needs to be done very frequently	• Is the intended audience reading the tweets? • Are they re-tweeting them? • How many followers do I have?	• Are the tweets communicating the right information? • Are they the right length? • Do they have the right frequency?
Provide in-depth analysis on subject area to demonstrate knowledge	Blog	One hour, once per week	Moderate, provided subject area is carefully chosen	• How many followers do I have? • Ask audience what else they would like to see covered	• Are people leaving comments or asking questions?
Keep connected to audience and appear personable	Facebook	10–15 minutes, twice per week	Minimal. Keep relevant photos and information in separate folder ready to use	• How many followers do I have? • Are they "liking" my status/posts?	• Are people leaving posts in reply? • Are they favourable? • Are they involved in any discussions?

Data management

This covers a large topic including diaries and to-do management lists which we have already looked at in terms of how best to use them to aid your productivity (see Chapter 8). But how do you decide which ones to invest in? The number and variety of such systems available to you is vast and can be bewildering, with something to suit every taste and need, but whichever you think might work best for you there are a few pointers which are worth bearing in mind.

DIARIES

▶ These should have a **quick view facility** to enable you to switch speedily between day, week and month layouts.

- They should include the ability to **jump directly into a full-day view** from any layout and to add, delete or alter entries.

- They should have the facility to **add notes** to any entry.

- They should allow **automatic entry from other applications** (e.g. emails).

- They should **automatically update** across all your systems which carry your diary (e.g. computer, phone, tablet, etc.).

TO-DO LISTS

- These should contain **easy-access day-by-day pages** with plenty of space to add notes etc.

- They should have a section devoted to **'today's tasks'** as well as a diary.

- They should contain the facility to **add projects** with multiple layers.

- They should contain a log of your **completed tasks,** with dates.

- They should **automatically update** across all your systems which carry your to-do list (e.g. computer, phone, tablet, etc.).

Used efficiently your diary and to-do list should work in harmony, providing a seamless and responsive scheduling system – an invaluable resource in the quest to boost your productivity.

INFORMATION STORAGE

The other key data-management area is that of your long-term information storage (e.g. a hard drive), and one of the most productivity-damaging occurrences which can affect your work life is a hard drive failure without the safety net of an external backup. Even in the short term these can be hugely damaging to your productivity since the loss of a week's work, or even a day's, means that all the time and effort you put in has counted for nothing with all the information irrevocably lost. In other words, all the time you spent creating the content which has now been lost was 100 per cent unproductive. In the long term it can be more damaging still since you may have irrevocably lost information which was crucial to the ongoing productivity of a project and which can never be replaced.

Fortunately, this can be easily avoided by implementing a backup routine for your data. This is one area where lazy people really do take the most pains, so in order to safeguard any work you have done, and thereby safeguard your productivity, you need to ensure that you have a robust process in place for backing up all of your work all of the time. There are, of course, myriad ways to store data but the crucial aspect is to ensure you have a ready-made backup of everything you have on your hard drive so that you never find yourself in the business-stalling situation of a mid-project data loss.

One option is to have a **server** which not only stores all your information in a location other than your computer's hard drive but also allows you to access it remotely. This can be a godsend if you find that you need to refer to or work on a piece of work which you have forgotten to take with you. A simpler and cheaper alternative is an **external hard drive.** Fortunately, these are now relatively low-cost for even very sizeable hard drives and most come with a basic dedicated software package to make backing up your data a simple and quick process. Many will even have an automatic backup feature, allowing the external hard drive to access and copy all the selected data from your computer automatically at pre-determined intervals defined by the user, ensuring you never need to remember to do it manually which can prove a real lifesaver.

Either way, you need to ensure that your external hard drive is backed up very frequently; it is, after all, only ever as up to date as you keep it and an out of date backup is of limited value. So set up your external hard drive to automatically back up your data at frequent intervals or make sure you are ultra-disciplined in doing so yourself to ensure that your productivity is never unnecessarily and damagingly hindered.

Quick fix: Back up your data now!

A complete copy of the latest state of your hard drive really is one of those things you never fully appreciate until you need it – only then do you discover its true value. So in order to safeguard any work you have done and therefore to safeguard your productivity, make sure you do not wait until you suffer a data loss – by which time it is too late – but get set up with a suitable backup system today.

The minimum requirement

The extent to which you need to be always accessible to your clients, and the degree to which you will need to have an unending capability to access them, your diary, your other business contacts, suppliers, the World Wide Web, etc. will of course depend on the nature and profile of your business but for almost everyone there is a minimum requirement of information technology which will need to be embraced. The trick is to ensure that whatever you choose to use they are tools which genuinely allow you to be more productive (e.g. by freeing up your time, by reaching a wider audience, by communicating with several people at once) and that you continually review their efficacy.

Correctly managed, the tools at your disposal can really boost your productivity as well as your efficiency and help to project an image of accessibility and professionalism. We are truly in the age of instant-access, instant-response, 24/7 zero-downtime connectivity which, used appropriately, can provide never-before-dreamed-of levels of accessibility, connectivity, communications and information delivery.

Conversely, a failure to fully embrace the information technology at your disposal or – equally damaging – a failure to employ suitable workplace practices to manage it appropriately, is to create a completely unnecessary and avoidable roadblock to productivity. By devoting up front the time and effort required to put in place the systems which will best serve you, you will almost certainly save yourself far more time and effort in the future, so getting it right really is time well spent. Remember that you may not get it right first time, so be prepared to review and revise your systems as you go along, keeping your diary always up to date and your to-do lists as short as possible.

'My to-do list is so long that it doesn't have an end; it has an event horizon.'

Craig Bruce

Next step

In this chapter we focused on the potential and pitfalls of information technology for our work-related productivity. In the final chapter we will look at some of the main barriers that stop us from reaching our full productivity.

10

Barriers to Productivity – and How to Overcome them

In this chapter you will learn how to:

▶ *Keep your to-do lists short and the entries prioritized*

▶ *Minimize distractions and disturbances*

▶ *Create the workplace environment which best suits your personality, your preferred working style and the needs of your current project*

▶ *Implement robust workplace security measures*

▶ *Create an adverse weather plan – be prepared for sudden and unexpected changes in the weather or extreme conditions.*

How do you feel?

1 Are you easily distracted? Are there obvious distractions which impair your productivity?

2 Do you prevaricate and waste time? Do you ever simply push work around instead of dealing with it?

3 Do you get a sufficient quality and quantity of stimulus in your work life?

4 Would silence and solitude enable you to get more done?

5 Do you have a robust and reliable system for ensuring that all of your work is protected from productivity-crippling loss or damage?

In the quest for maximizing your productivity it is essential that you identify any habits you may have formed, or areas of your work life, which are hindering you. You need to be able to function at your most effective for the longest stretches of time possible, deftly weaving economy of effort with the largest gains and – crucially – eliminating anything which gets in the way. Let's take a look at some of the most common productivity impairing workplace habits.

Avoiding prevarication and transference

It is time to put the monkey back on your shoulder. Most of us write to-do lists of the required tasks for the day/week/year ahead. It is a great way of getting organized, and prioritizing our workload; and there is a wonderful sense of satisfaction in completing the tasks and then crossing them off the list. However – and it is a big 'however' – this works only if the lists and the timeframes are kept short. Making long lists of things you plan to achieve is a fantastic way of ensuring you never do. Quite simply, long lists = transference; and transference = getting nowhere fast.

THE 'TRANSFERENCE TRAP'

This is the 'transference trap'. Compiling lists may make you feel better, but what does it actually achieve? Without proper management, very little; worse – it fools you into feeling that you are making great strides when in reality you are barely toddling.

'Reorganizing can be a wonderful method for creating the illusion of progress while producing confusion, inefficiency, and demoralization.'

Petronius Arbiter

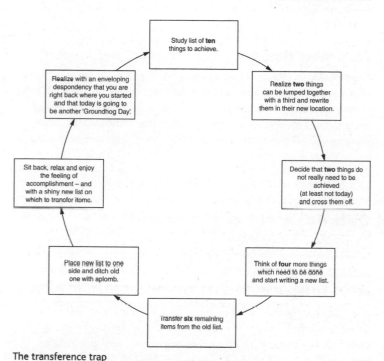

The transference trap

AVOIDING THE TRAP

Follow these simple rules in order to avoid the transference trap:

▶ Keep your lists **short** and **relevant.**

▶ Ensure they only include tasks which really are **achievable.**

▶ **Prioritize** them and work from the **top down,** focusing on just one task at a time.

- Make sure that you **see each task through to completion** before moving on to the next.

Remember that simply writing the lists themselves accomplishes nothing, and that compiling an endless series of lists is a recipe for productivity failure since the very act of writing them gives you a false sense of reassurance that the tasks have been accomplished.

Remember this: Keep your lists short and concise

By keeping your lists short and to the point, it is easier to see at a glance what needs to be done and to ensure that you actually do it. A good habit to get into is to prioritize each item you add to your list at the time of entry. In this way, you can always work from the top of your list down knowing you are completing the tasks in the best order without having to reread the entire list each time.

Quick fix: Create a list template

If you prefer to keep your lists on screen rather than on paper, it can be advantageous to devote the necessary time to creating a template. Although this takes time in the first place it can save you a lot of time later on, not only because you will always have a blank pro forma ready to hand but also because you will become extremely familiar with the layout allowing you to navigate it quickly and easily.

Avoiding distractions and disturbances

'Work is hard. Distractions are plentiful. And time is short.'
Adam Hochschild

Distractions are indeed plentiful and each one is a ready-made opportunity to lose valuable time and momentum, hindering your productivity. The trick is to avoid them in the first place and to do this you will need to do the following:

- Understand **where** any workplace distractions **are likely to come from.**

- Be **ever alert** to the possibility of distractions and see them coming.

- Know **in advance** what you will do to combat them.

- Have in place the **necessary mechanisms** to facilitate this.

- Always keep handy an **instant reminder** of why you want to avoid the distraction (e.g. an incentive for finishing the work you are doing).

- Determine **measurement criteria** to enable you to judge the efficacy of your mechanisms.

- Periodically **review and revise.**

It is particularly important to review your situation while being alert to the possibility of distractions having crept into your work life 'under the radar'. It is very easy to get into routines in which distractions have become commonplace and therefore accepted – indeed, they may no longer be seen as distractions at all. And the longer they are permitted to remain, the more difficult it will be to see them for what they really are – hindrances to your productivity – and more difficult to combat them. So try to get into the habit of reviewing your situation with a 360-degree perspective in mind.

Quick fix: Be prepared

Many of the disturbances and disruptions to which you may be susceptible can be seen coming if you know where to look. By determining *where*, and if possible *when*, these are likely to occur, you can put in place coping mechanisms well in advance to minimize their effects, and thereby minimize their ability to impair your productivity.

Working from home

The challenge of combatting distractions is even harder for the solo worker, and doubly so for everyone who works from home. We are magnets to a myriad of time-wasting sidetracks and unproductive cul-de-sacs, and if distractions do not find us we will all too often find them – or even create them. And just to make life really difficult, they are not always easy to spot. Indeed, some of the most pernicious can appear totally benign, or even helpful.

Let us take an example – housework. It is all too easy to notice a cobweb in the corner of your office or some dust on a filing cabinet and to dispatch yourself there and then to put the matter in hand. After all, surely that is just good housekeeping? En route to getting the vacuum cleaner or duster and polish, you notice some crockery which needs loading into the dishwasher, a pile of washing waiting to be done (and then ironed), and that you are nearly out of milk. Not to mention the dripping tap that needs seeing to, and the windows which need cleaning, and ... Before you know it the working day will have become the evening and you will be no further forward with your work than you were before breakfast.

It is incredibly easy to be distracted in this way and just about everyone who works from home is guilty of it from time to time, but it is a real trap and a real time-waster. So how do you combat it? First and foremost you need to stay focused on the fact that while you might be in your house you are not at home – you are at work, in the office. Try to imagine that you are working in a busy office and apply the rules and working practices which would be right for that environment. Would you really put aside the project on which you were working to suddenly grab the vacuum cleaner from the cleaners' cupboard or equip yourself with a mop and bucket and set about cleaning your office? Exactly. And if it would not be acceptable there, in a shared office while you were at work, then it should not be acceptable when you work from home, in the office while you are at work.

Quite simply, while you are at work, work. Vacuuming, dusting, doing the washing, feeding the cat, loading the dishwasher, unloading the dishwasher, shopping for the evening meal – whatever it is you are tempted to do, if it would not fit the day-to-day working life of a large multinational then leave it.

Not allowing yourself to get bogged down in this way begins with not allowing yourself to give in to even one distraction since the first one leads to another and then another and so on. They are all chores which are necessary evils but they are chores which are part of your home life not your work life, which means they can wait – can and *must* – until you get home from work, not physically but mentally.

Disturbances are also plentiful, whether they are self-imposed or from external sources. While they can largely be grouped under the heading of 'Distractions' they are worth noting in their own right as they also include such things as:

- other people in your work life interrupting your work
- other people in your home life interrupting your work
- IT malfunctions interrupting your work
- unexpected demands on your time (from bosses, new pieces of work to be readied, etc.)
- holidays (including bank holidays)
- unexpected absences from work (e.g. owing to illness, transport strikes, etc.)
- absences from work for other people in your team.

Each of these has the potential to be damaging to your productivity (and this list is by no means exhaustive), but by keeping a weather eye out for any likely disturbances you can at least minimize their impact.

Isolation and company as barriers to productivity

We have already seen that socializing instead of working can lead to a sharp downturn in productivity, but perhaps less obvious is the fact that isolation can have just the same effect. This is for several reasons:

- the need for **stimulation**
- the desire for **external input**

- the desire for **extra stimulus**
- the need for **company**.

This, of course, causes something of a conundrum: both having company and not having company can lead to an impairment in productivity! On the other hand, both having company and not having company can lead to an *increase* in productivity – the key is to find the right balance, and that can be a very personal thing. Some people thrive with a lot of company and need to find those times when shutting themselves off to the outside world is going to help them to focus and concentrate and then be sure to force themselves to do it in order to boost their productivity. Others flourish when left to their own devices in a quiet, people-free environment and need to realize when their productivity would be boosted by exposing themselves to the stimulus which being around other people can provide. In order to use this to help you to function at your maximum productivity level, you will need to determine:

- which of these groups you fit into (although most people find they are somewhere between the two extremes)
- how you will get the company/alone time
- how you will achieve getting the right balance for you.

If you work in a shared workplace, then the biggest challenge may well be finding space to be alone. If you work alone, then the biggest challenge will almost certainly be finding the necessary stimulus as and when you need it. Either way, finding the right balance and determining ways to implement it are crucial to ensuring you have the best possible chance of functioning at your maximum productivity level for the maximum amount of time.

> 'If isolation tempers the strong, it is the stumbling-block of the uncertain.'
>
> Paul Cezanne

HOW TO FIND ISOLATION IN A SHARED WORK ENVIRONMENT
Some companies have realized the need for periods of isolation for their employees and have installed 'silent rooms' or 'quiet

time areas'. These, as their names suggest, are places where people can go to reap the benefits of silence or near silence, allowing them to work undisturbed and to concentrate fully on the task at hand without fear of distraction. Typically these venues are:

- soundproofed and/or away from noisy areas
- used only for solo work (i.e. never used for meetings etc.)
- free from telephones and have a 'no mobiles' policy
- neutrally decorated.

Some also block Internet access.

Such places are a great solution and have the added benefit of helping to ensure that you won't be disturbed by colleagues since the question of 'Where is so and so?' will be met with the answer that they are in the silent room, which instantly implies that they do not wish to be disturbed – this is usually enough to ensure that the person who wishes to find them will wait until a more suitable time.

If you are not fortunate enough to have use of such a facility, however, you will need to be more creative. Some of the venues which workers seeking solitude have used to enable them to find peace and quiet include:

- meeting rooms
- conference rooms
- stairwells
- shower rooms (provided mainly for people cycling to work but seldom used once work is underway)
- local libraries
- their car in the car park!

Wherever you can find a space is fine, but it is a good idea to get into the habit of letting your colleagues know that this is why you are disappearing for a while so that they will know not to disturb you. You might even prefer to tell them that you are going out for a while but not tell them where you are going!

HOW TO FIND COMPANY IF YOU WORK ALONE

For many people who work alone two of the major hindrances to their productivity are:

1 the lack of a **social element** to their work life

2 **the inability to seek ideas, reassurance, moan about something, celebrate a success,** etc. during the working day.

Countering this requires some ingenuity but it well worth the effort as it really can help to boost your productivity.

Loneliness can be a major barrier to productivity for those who work alone and never if this more keenly felt than during the downtimes in the working day. While you are hard at work, you will probably be too busy working to notice or care, but as soon as you take a break, particularly your lunch break, you may well find the silence to be deafening and, whereas in a shared working environment people may well go out for lunch with some colleagues, you instead find yourself stuck in an isolated working environment, alone.

In order to counter this, take a moment to think about a shared working environment and think back to when you worked in a shared environment, or when you were at university or college: Did you sit at your desk every day to eat your lunch? Or did you go out somewhere, at least every once in a while, perhaps to a local restaurant or café, or to get some takeout sandwiches from a good deli to eat in the park and enjoy a change of scene. Maybe you would go with a colleague or two and try to talk about anything but work, or even if you did find the conversation wandering back to the company, perhaps it was to gossip, not to discuss work plans. And on those occasions when you did stay in the office building you were probably keen to at least make sure that you got away from your desk for some of your break – to the canteen, common room, lounge, etc.

So what is the difference now? You may work alone but that does not have to mean that you never meet anyone for lunch. You may work from home but that does not mean that you cannot ever leave it. If you craved a social element to your working life before, then you almost certainly need it just as much now – so make sure you get it. One of the disadvantages to working alone is that it will take more time and effort to engineer, so it is probably not practical to try to do it every day but you should certainly be able to find time to go out and meet someone for lunch at least once a week. Use it as a natural opportunity to network, affording you the opportunity to boost your productivity not only by enjoying some company but also by seeing how you might be able to grow your business. And you might even be able to claim it as a business expense!

On those occasions when you will have to enjoy your own company there is still no reason not to get out and enjoy a change of scene. A good idea is to train yourself to engage in distractions (watch television, read a book, listen to some music) and mentally move out of the workplace. Of course, you will need to be disciplined to avoid taking breaks when you should be working and this can be a difficult habit to get used to – but so can forcing yourself to take breaks when you *should* and this really is crucial in allowing yourself the space to boost your productivity.

Remember this: Don't take advantage of your situation

Although there are many advantages to working alone which you should enjoy to the full and leverage to maximize your productivity – not least the flexibility it affords in your work life – it is all too easy to take advantage of your situation to the *detriment* of your work. A good rule of thumb for what is and what is not appropriate is to think about a large multinational and see whether whatever behaviour or action you are considering would be considered acceptable or advantageous there. If it would, then it is probably going to be good for your work, too; if it would not, then you need to think long and hard about your reasons for wanting to do it before committing yourself.

Workplace discipline and security

Your workplace productivity can be impaired by a lax approach to discipline and to the security of your system and processes, so ensuring that these are sufficient and robust is key. Implementing a strict regime of workplace discipline and good practice in order to ensure that you can function at your maximum capacity all the time with no attendant loss of productivity is crucial to safeguarding your efficiency and limiting the possibility of costly infrastructure meltdowns. You will need to put in place rigorous safeguards to:

► prevent **data loss**

► prevent **data theft**

► prevent **malicious damage**

► prevent costly (in time and resources) **system failures**

► ensure that you are not faced with **prolonged periods of inactivity**

► streamline your working **practices**

► achieve maximum **efficiency**

► **boost your productivity.**

Many of the safeguards you need to employ and the good habits which you need to make routine in your day-to-day working life will already be in place if you are employed by a large company since they will have robust measures in place to protect you and your work, many of which do not involve your direct input. Indeed, you may not even be aware of their presence.

If, however, the buck for everything stops with you, you will need to assume responsibility for the security of your work as well as that of your clients on those occasions when you are made privy to sensitive data.

 Try it now: Protect your data

If you have any data in your possession, whether on paper or on disk, it is in all probability your responsibility to protect it. If you work for yourself and such data falls into the wrong hands, you may well be held accountable and liable to face the consequences for any damage which occurs as a result. The same can also apply if you work for someone else since it is often made the responsibility of the individual employees to safeguard any information in their possession. You will therefore need to ascertain what processes are available at your place of work or, if you work alone, you will need to put such processes in place.

One of the simplest processes which can be established is to shred all documents at source as soon as they are no longer needed. Many companies employ a firm to dispose securely of all documents, disks, etc. but if you work for yourself you will need to invest in a shredder. You may well already have one for domestic purposes but in terms of security you need to ensure that the shredder you use for your business is located in your office and used only by you. You also need to make sure that it is man enough for the job – that is, it must be a crosscut shredder so that materials are not simply cut vertically into long thin strips but are also cut horizontally so that any sensitive hard-copy data is quickly transformed into tiny, meaningless short shreds, and it must also be able to cope with more than just paper, for those occasions when you need to dispose of card, celluloid, etc. This has the additional benefit of allowing you to shred thin sheet data in large quantities.

If you expect to have a lot of data of which you need to dispose then it is also advisable to invest in a shredder whose receptacle capacity negates the need to empty it every five minutes as this will only deter you from shredding everything which you know ought to be shredded and slow you down, damaging your productivity.

Finally, a shredder in your office is a permanent presence and a constant reminder to keep on top of your paperwork and prevent it turning into a paper mountain, to clear the decks on a regular basis. This will free you up to concentrate on the important things and boost your productivity.

'Throw the lumber over, man! Let your boat of life be light...'
Jerome K. Jerome

In the same way that you need to keep your desk cleared of the sea of paperwork which will otherwise threaten to drown you, so you need to treat your hard drive in much the same way. By deleting any data which is no longer required you will keep on top of security while at the same time freeing up your hard drive. This will boost your productivity by:

- making it **quicker to search** for and open pieces of work

- keep your **thoughts streamlined** by dispensing with all unnecessary items

- keep the **focus** of your efforts where it should be

- prevent you from feeling the need to **periodically go through everything** on your hard drive.

Remember this: Data never entirely disappears

Do not forget that deleting information from your computer and even formatting the hard drive does not get rid of the data; instead, it simply tells your computer that this information is no longer required and the areas in which it is stored can now be used. Thus, the data which you have deleted will remain on your hard drive until it is overwritten. If you want to remove it permanently from your computer you will need to use a program which wipes it clean to 'factory new' status.

On the other side of the coin is the need to ensure that all work is properly protected from corruption or unwanted deletion and that it is securely backed up. If you work for a large company, this may be performed for you automatically, but be sure to see exactly what is and isn't included with any data backups – often it is only the information stored on computers, which leaves every other storage media vulnerable. If you work alone, then it is highly likely that you will need to take full responsibility for backing up your data.

Quick fix: Check what's included

If you think that at least a portion of your data is backed up remotely on your behalf, be sure to find out exactly what is and isn't included. Then make sure that you fill any gaps. If you are in the habit, for instance, of storing data in your mobile phone, then check that it is included in your company backup. If it isn't (and it probably isn't), then the onus will be on you to perform regular backups.

This really is an area in which lazy people take the most pains, as anyone will know who has ever had a computer crash terminally with an irrevocable loss of data, or suffered the loss of a PDA, mobile phone, etc. or had one freeze necessitating a complete reformatting and the resulting loss of all the contents, including all contact details. There are few eventualities which can befall you which are so damaging to your productivity, and often people do not realize just how important the information is and how lost they would be without it until it is too late. Worse still, an irretrievable loss of data could mean an inability to complete a piece of work for a client, resulting in a loss of revenue and sharply diminishing your prospects of ever being asked to work for them again. Happily, the answer is simple and straightforward and the process is easy to accomplish. The only tricky bit is remembering to do it!

To back up a computer you will need to invest in an external hard drive onto which you can write all necessary data, and you should get into the habit of doing this on a regular basis. Exactly how often will depend on the speed and regularity at which you gather and store new information; for some people it is a task which needs to be undertaken every few minutes; for others it is sufficient to do it every few hours, for others once per day/week, etc. The same principle goes for any other devices on which you store information.

Remember this: Back up at least once a week

Whatever your line of work, try to ensure that you back up your hard drive and any other data storage devices at least once per week. This really should be the maximum length of time you leave it because getting into the habit of backing up your data regularly is the only way to ensure it never gets forgotten, overlooked or postponed until it is too late causing a potentially disastrous loss – both of data and productivity.

Surely the easiest way to ensure your data is protected is to utilize the automatic backup software with which most external hard drives, mobile phones, etc. come. This enables them to automatically back up a specified hard drive, server, etc. once you have determined the regularity with which you wish this task to be performed. Utilizing this option is an excellent way to ensure that the task always gets done, and on time, although the operation can be intrusive and puts extra demands on the processor (and can be noisy, too), so make sure that you bear this in mind when determining the days and times at which you want this to occur.

 Try it now: Use a memory stick

If you just need to back up a small amount of data on an ad hoc basis, it can be useful to use an extra, smaller storage device such as a USB flash drive (sometimes called a USB memory stick). This operation is usually much quicker than using an external hard drive to perform a full backup and brings with it the benefit of portability. It can also act as a second backup storage device for any vitally important data. This belt-and-braces approach can work well if you get into the habit of backing up the projects on which you are currently working to both storage devices. Just remember to keep them in separate locations.

Since a data loss will almost certainly mean a loss of productivity, ensuring that it never happens is the safest way to safeguarding your productivity. As well is backing up all your important data it is a good idea to get into the habit of giving your computer a weekly 'spring-clean'. Whether you do this at the same time as backing up your data, or whether you prefer to keep these tasks separate (particularly if you have set up the 'fire and forget' automatic backup to run during the night), giving your computer a regular service will help to keep it running at its most efficient allowing your productivity to do the same. Obviously, the number and nature of the tasks required will vary from business to business but there are three key tasks which you should always try to accomplish as a minimum:

1 **Update any virus protection software you have installed**
The requirements for this are largely dependent on the operating system you use and to some extent the number and nature of Internet searches your business requires you to make, but whatever your situation it is worth erring on the side of caution. It is certainly better to have too

much protection than too little since the consequences of a malware invasion on your system can be devastating to your productivity. Keeping on top of the latest software threats on a regular basis is your best defence. Those who get their kicks writing malicious software never take a week off, so neither should you.

2 **Defragment your hard drives and empty any unwanted cache, folders, etc.** Keeping your system clean in this way not only helps to make it easier to navigate your hard drives and to see where things are at a glance but it will also improve your system's speed and efficiency. Not developing good habits in this respect will impair your system over time, making you less efficient and less productive. Another benefit to regular defragmentation of your hard drives is an increase in their storage capacity.

3 **Ensure you know where everything on your computer is and revisit any folders whose contents you are unsure of or which you had forgotten about completely!** This is an area which is often overlooked in the busy work routines of modern office life but it is a great way to boost your productivity with relatively little effort. Even the most efficient of people will find that getting into this routine sometimes produces unexpected results and having a firm grasp of where everything is just when you need it can save a lot of wasted time – vital when you have no time to waste.

Case study

'It wasn't until I went through my hard drives for the first time, carefully checking all my folders and subfolders, that I realized just how much was there that I'd forgotten about, or didn't remember ever knowing. It took me a couple of days because I had left it so long and it was boring, tedious work, but the results proved well worth it because I came across folders I'd long since forgotten about – and in some cases, clients! I immediately set about making amends, more clearly labelling folders and putting them where they should be, and contacting the clients I had rediscovered. Now I go through this process every Friday morning to ensure I don't make the same mistakes again and it only takes me about 20 minutes...'

Eliminating procrastination and avoidance

Procrastination and avoidance are two enemies of productivity which it is all too easy to allow into your work life – indeed, they often creep in unnoticed or under the guise of something worthwhile. How often have you been guilty of deferring something which you know you ought to get on with because it seems like too much hard work? Common reasons for procrastination and avoidance include:

▶ the work is **boring**

▶ time pressures are **not urgent** (or do not exist)

▶ the work is **hard**

▶ the work is **unrewarding**

▶ you think **someone else might do it** if you leave it

▶ it can be **deferred until a later date.**

The problem with all of these reasons – well, *excuses* – is that they are damaging to your productivity since they usually merely put off the inevitable until a later date and until the work is done it is left hanging over you, a constant irritation and a drain on your resources. Getting the work done as soon as possible is the best route to boosting your productivity because:

▶ the work won't just go away – it will still **need to be done** at some point

▶ until it is done it will be a **constant nagging thorn in your side**

▶ you may be **less able to complete the work later** (e.g. because you are busier or unwell)

▶ all the time the work remains unfinished (or not even started) it **draws a part of your focus**

▶ **your resources are finite** – do not allow them to be depleted unnecessarily

- completing work early gives you a sense of **making progress**

- completing work early may be **beneficial to your colleagues, clients,** etc.

- the work may **take longer to complete** than you had allowed.

Myth-buster

'It doesn't matter when the work is done as long as it gets done.' This is untrue because completing work early not only carries the advantages listed above but also gets you into an excellent time-management routine which is necessary in order to boost your productivity. It also gives your colleagues, customers and clients confidence in your ability and determination to complete work ahead of schedule.

One way to boost your productivity is by turning things on their head and deliberately doing the hardest and least enjoyable things first. In this way, you:

- **get them out of the way** as soon as possible

- ensure you **don't have to keep thinking about them**

- **free yourself up** for other work

- ensure you have the **more enjoyable/rewarding work** to do next

- **manage your time** to best advantage.

Coping with extreme weather conditions

It is amazing just how many work hours are lost every year to the vagaries of the weather. Typically, these include any sudden or unexpected weather conditions and can easily impair productivity if they are not guarded against. Although no one can plan for every eventuality, it's a good idea to be as prepared as you can be. Draw up a table such as the one below, listing all the likely adverse weather conditions which might disrupt your ability to operate at your maximum productivity levels, how you might be affected and what you can do to combat it.

Type of weather	How this might affect your productivity	What you can do to minimize the disruption
Snow	Inability to get to work	Take measures to work from home
Heat wave	Physically draining	Install some temporary air conditioning
Hurricane	Unsafe to travel	Take measures to work from home
Flooding	Usual routes or transport method unavailable	Research alternative modes of transport and/ or routes
Extreme cold	Disruption to rail services	Leave extra time to get to and from work or arrange to travel by other means

Next step

Throughout this book we have looked at some of the habits, pitfalls and problems that can frustrate and hinder our productivity. What I have tried to do is to provide you with a toolkit of techniques and ideas that can help you boost your productivity and – hopefully – to achieve a better work/life balance. The next step – deploying the toolkit in a way that best suits you and your situation – is down to you!

Index